I Love Mondays

The autobiography of Alec Reed

Alec Reed, Serial Entrepreneur

Businesses
Reed Employment
  (1960)
Reed Executive (1961)
D. Eyre & Partners
  (1963)
Club Pass (1966)
ICC (Inter Company
  Comparisons) (1967)
Dial a Job (1968)
Medicare (1973)
reed.co.uk (1995)
Reed in Partnership
  (1998)

Charities
Reed Business School
  (1972)
Addicts Rehabilitation
  (1973)
Womankind (1989)
Ethiopiaid (1989)
Reed Re-start (1995)
West London Academy
  (2002)
The Big Give (2007)

I Love Mondays

The autobiography of Alec Reed

Alec Reed

with Judi Bevan

PROFILE BOOKS

First published in Great Britain in 2012 by
Profile Books Ltd
3a Exmouth House
Pine Street
Exmouth Market
London EC1R 0JH
www.profilebooks.com

10 9 8 7 6 5 4 3 2 1

A CIP catalogue record for this book is available from the British Library.

ISBN: 978 1 84668 516 3
eISBN: 978 1 84765 767 1

Text design by Sue Lamble
sue@lambledesign.demon.co.uk
Typeset in Photina by MacGuru Ltd
info@macguru.org.uk

Printed and bound in Great Britain by
Clays, Bungay, Suffolk

The paper this book is printed on is certified by the © 1996 Forest Stewardship
Council A.C. (FSC). It is ancient-forest friendly. The printer holds FSC chain of
custody SGS-COC-2061

FSC
Mixed Sources
Product group from well-managed
forests and other controlled sources
Cert no. SGS-COC-2061
www.fsc.org
© 1996 Forest Stewardship Council

Contents

To Adrianne, my soulmate.

And to Rosie, Tessa, Harry, Patrick, Joe, Hazel,
Aidan, Molly, Tabitha, Lily, Christie
and their parents.

Occupied in these reflections, as he was making his way along one of the great public thoroughfares of London, he chanced to raise his eyes to a blue board, whereon was inscribed, in characters of gold, 'General Agency Office; for places and situations of all kinds inquire within'. It was a shop-front, fitted up with a gauze blind and an inner door; and in the window hung a long and tempting array of written placards, announcing vacant places of every grade, from a secretary's to a foot-boy's. Nicholas halted, instinctively before this temple of promise ... he made up his mind and stepped in.

From *Nicholas Nickleby* by Charles Dickens

Chronology

16 February 1934: Born in Hounslow
1950: Starts work at Tozer, Kemsley and Milbourn
1954: Qualifies as a Chartered Secretary
1955: Joins Gillette
May 1960: Opens first employment agency
16 September 1961: Marries Adrianne Eyre
1963: Qualifies as a Chartered Management Accountant
January 1971: Floats Reed Executive on Stock Exchange
1972: Founds Reed Charity, forerunner of Reed
    Foundation; starts Reed Business School; number of
    Reed branches hits 100
1973: Turnover tops £10 million for first time; AR
    launches Medicare chain of drug stores
1977: Reed profits top £1 million for first time
1985: Sells Medicare to Dee Corporation for £20 million
1987: Visits Ethiopia for first time; made Professor of
    Enterprise and Innovation at Royal Holloway College,
    University of London
1989: Founds Ethiopiaid and Womankind charities
1993: Honoured as a fellow of CIPD (Chartered Institute
    of Personnel and Development)
1994: Awarded CBE

1995: Launches reed.co.uk, internet recruitment site
1995: Starts Reed Learning in Windsor
1997: Son James Reed becomes chief executive
1998: Reed in Partnership launched
1999: Profits top £20 million for first time; AR becomes
    'Founder at Large'
2002: Publishes *Capitalism Is Dead: Peoplism Rules*
2003: Reed Executive taken private
2005: Reed Health bought back into Reed Executive
2007: Launches The Big Give, internet charity site
2011: Receives Knight Bachelor for services to business
    and charity

Prologue

I HAVE ALWAYS HAD A HEAD FULL OF IDEAS. My brain is like one of those machines that shoot balls into the air at fairgrounds. Some of those balls get caught and win prizes: others just fall to the ground. Every day for more than fifty years I have come up with something. Many of my ideas were trivial and silly and didn't come to much, but enough of them did. Opening my first employment agency was like backing a roulette number and it coming up. That happens rarely, but in business, if you get an idea right, the winning number keeps coming up. From the moment I opened my first employment agency I never missed my salary from Gillette, where I had worked for four years. Gillette became my first client, and gave me back that salary many times over in fees.

People often ask me what made me entrepreneurial. Was it growing up amid the uncertainty of war, when you never knew if the next doodlebug was going to fall on you or if the next air raid would be your last? I don't think so. Millions of children lived through those experiences and did not become entrepreneurs. The war made most people risk averse; they wanted secure jobs in big firms with good wages and guaranteed pensions – and there were plenty of those jobs going in the two decades after the war. That is what made the recruitment business so profitable.

As a child my motivation mostly came from trying to keep up with my big brother John who was four years older than me. He was a big influence when we were younger. My mother was always separating us. If we were fighting, I was obviously going to get the worst of it ... eight versus four, or six against ten or whatever. But he led the way. He had an entrepreneurial streak fired by the desire to escape the financial constraints of our childhood. I desperately wanted to keep up with him. As I grew older, I had a burning desire to show that I was as good as him.

I was five when the war started, and the hardships and excitement certainly encouraged John and me to be enterprising. Our first venture was making and selling lead soldiers. Then we started another little business, personalising greetings cards. I don't remember being competitive about my schoolwork but I have always wanted to win whatever game I played, whether tennis or cards.

Even more compelling than the will to win has been the need to be in control of my own destiny. That is what made me leave my safe, well-paid job at Gillette when I was 26. While the management welcomed some of the ideas that popped out of my head I had no control over what happened to them. When I left I had only two goals – first to run my own business, and second to make enough money to equal my salary of £900 a year.

The ambition to expand the business, to overtake my rivals and become the market leader, came later.

Plenty of people have good ideas, but they never follow them through because they lack energy or confidence. My parents – my mother in particular – gave us tons of confidence by always taking our side. I like people, so I have never had trouble getting on with those around me and confidence helped me to persuade them to do things my way.

Thanks to my mother's unconditional support, I always saw the glass half full – even when things went wrong. I never minded rejection so knocking on doors or approaching people with an idea or a product held little fear. I tried many things that have failed, such as turning the employment agencies into record shops on a Saturday or branching out into Phone a Job in the United States. I have learned a lot through failure. I know that if an idea does not work it is simply the idea that fails, not me as a person. So I can always shrug it off and get going again.

My management style is straightforward. I like to take people with me, not terrorise them into doing what I think is right. I am not judgemental, but if colleagues or suppliers do not deliver what they promise, I am quite direct about telling them. I will fire those who don't come up to scratch although I have always tried to do it humanely.

Above all I believe that a sense of humour is vital. Many of my ideas have been about making work fun. If people laugh while they are working, if there is a buzz in the office, if they are excited and challenged, they work harder. Someone once asked me if I managed by fear, like some well-known entrepreneurs. 'No,' I said, 'I prefer laughter.'

CHAPTER 1

---

96 Rosemary Avenue

MY FIRST MEMORY is of the day Britain declared war on Germany. On that sunny Sunday morning on 3 September 1939 my parents, my elder brother John and I had come in from the garden to listen to the Prime Minister on an old Bakelite wireless. I was five, yet instinctively I sensed the tension in the room and knew something momentous was happening. I can still remember the sombre tone of Neville Chamberlain's voice as he said those famous words: 'As a result, this country is at war with Germany.' In what seemed like seconds after the broadcast ended, the air raid sirens wailed. It was the most chilling sound I had ever heard.

My mother, along with many others, thought the Gestapo would be marching up the street within hours. She panicked, as did our next-door neighbours, a Czech refugee family who I think were Jewish. The husband was a tailor by trade and amazingly owned the only car on the estate, a grey Vauxhall – an object of great fascination to John and me.

Within the hour, my mother, John and I all piled into the car and fled the Germans with them! My father, who had fought in the First World War, stayed calm and just let us go. In the 'war to end all wars' he had been a sergeant in the trenches with the Warwickshire Regiment, although he rarely talked about it. In later life I visited both Ypres and the Somme, which brought home to me how lucky he was to have made it back; so many of the Warwickshire's sergeants did not. Somehow the experience made him quite fatalistic. My mother, on the other hand, thought only of her children's safety, so, crammed into that little car, we fled – I have little recollection where to. It might have been Henley.

We drove and drove and after a while the adults came to their senses, realised there was nowhere safe to flee to and that the Germans had not invaded. So they turned around and we were all back home for tea by about six o'clock. What a bizarre day!

After that dramatic beginning, no bombs fell on London for a further eight months – the period known as the 'Phoney War'. And then the Blitz began.

I was born on 16 February 1934 and was brought home to that same house, 96 Rosemary Avenue, in Hounslow, Middlesex. Apart from two years in the Army, I lived there until I married my wife Adrianne at 27.

It was a small, end-of-terrace house built in the late 1920s and typical of the outer London suburbs. There was no garage because there were hardly any cars then, but there was a wide alleyway at the side where briefly I once kept a horse. Every house had a lovingly tended little front garden and the council planted flowering cherry trees which scattered their petals along the street when the April breezes caught the branches.

Our house would have been worth just a few hundred pounds before the war. Today similar properties change hands for £250,000 – but the front gardens have gone, concreted over to make room for cars; the trees have also disappeared. Walking round the area now, it feels more desolate than it did in the war, even with rationing and regular air raids. I have written several letters to the council leader bemoaning its fate, but I guess he has a lot on his plate.

My father's name was Leonard – although my mother called him Jimmy. He was born in 1891 in Radford, a small village near Coventry. His parents, Isaac and Jane, had five daughters and four sons. My father was the second youngest in this large family; the youngest child was born when her eldest sister was 20. Growing up in rural Warwickshire gave him an abiding love of the countryside, which he passed on to me and John. After school he served an apprenticeship as a lithographic artist. In those days you were awarded the Freedom of Coventry if you completed your apprenticeship.

My parents had met in Carrickfergus outside Belfast. My maternal grandfather, who sadly I never met, had been posted there with his family. My father was stationed there after the First World War and I imagine my parents met at an Army dance. Strangely, they never spoke about it. They had a good marriage – we never heard a cross word between them.

By the time John and I were born, our father was working in HM Stationery Office as a middle-grade civil servant. Even so, he had bought his own home, stretching the finances to the limit. Like him, most of the other people in Rosemary Avenue were 'white collar' or office workers, although there were some families headed by what my parents called 'blue collar' workers. Today there is a huge ethnic mix with a pre-dominance of Asian families.

During the war there were hardly any cars so all the kids played in the street – games such as hopscotch, and cowboys and Indians – and there were plenty of scuffles. Hounslow West, at the end of the Piccadilly Line, was the nearest Tube station, connecting us to the rest of the world, particularly the excitement of central London.

During the Blitz – Hitler's attempt to destroy British morale – there were air raids almost every day. You never knew where the bombs would fall. Between September 1940 and May 1941 more than 43,000 civilians were killed in the South East in the most sustained period of bombing in the entire war. Although the East End of London got the worst of it, Rosemary Avenue was between Heston Airport and the Hounslow Cavalry barracks, both Nazi targets. Today there is even a street named Spitfire Way in Hounslow.

In May 1941 Hitler gave up trying to bomb Britain into submission and turned his attention to the Russian front. But even after that I don't remember it ever being peaceful. It seemed as though the Germans never took a holiday.

Even during the lulls we all lived in fear of air raids. The wardens would come round at night, yelling if they could see a chink of light. As I grew older, I led a group of boys who used to run wild over a nearby gravel pit that became a dumping ground for the wreckage of bombed houses. We called ourselves a gang but gangs were nothing like as violent as today. We used to play hide and seek in and around the air raid shelters and scavenge in the gravel pit like children in developing countries do today.

Of course we were scared during air raids, especially at

the beginning, but for a small boy the war was exciting. One day we found a dead baby in a shelter. It sounds gruesome, but we were rather proud of ourselves and, strangely, it gave us a bit of kudos with the other boys.

I was evacuated twice, but for only a few weeks when the bombing got really bad. On both occasions my parents made the arrangements; the trips were not part of the official evacuation programme, but we were still living with strangers even if they were relatives.

The first time was during the Blitz. John and I were both sent to some cousins in Ashby de la Zouch in Leicestershire. The second time I was sent on my own to a mining family in Ferndale, a small town in the Rhondda Valley. I stayed in a small miner's cottage to which the father would come home at night covered in coal dust. He would strip down and sit naked in a zinc bath in the kitchen while his wife and sometimes the children scrubbed him down. I was fascinated. Even more fascinating for a small boy was the sight of one of the older daughters breastfeeding her baby. I never knew where I was supposed to be looking.

While working as a lithographic artist at HM Stationery Office in Oxford Street, during the war, my father supervised the production of various posters and leaflets. One was the now-famous 'Keep calm and carry on' poster, but mostly they were propaganda leaflets to drop over Germany. He would bring home examples of pictures of tanks and heavily armed soldiers, designed to frighten German civilians.

I think we were more frightened by their bombs. Two houses in Rosemary Avenue suffered direct hits during the Blitz. Travelling up to town and back on the Tube every day, Dad must often have wondered if his house would still be standing when he got home. Luckily for all of us, it always was.

He had a good sense of humour, which I inherited. When the BBC radio programme 'Lift Up Your Hearts' came on at ten to eight each morning, he would call out 'Lift up your feet!' as he left for work.

He always stayed calm and even during air raids he never went into the Morrison shelter erected in the back room. It doubled as a perfect surface for table tennis. My mother was more frightened, although she tried not to show it in front of us. Even before we had the shelter she had made up beds for John and me under the stairs.

My father was 42 when I was born, and having done his stint in the First World War was too old to fight; but he was a member of the Home Guard in central London. Some nights he would stay in London to do his duties, which must have been very hard for my mother.

Most frightening were the flying V-1s, which the Nazis introduced towards the end of the war in 1944. They were known as buzz bombs, or doodlebugs, because of the distinctive noise they made when flying overhead. When the sound stopped, you knew the rocket was coming down.

As the war went on we became used to living with uncertainty and the ever-present threat of death, like most Londoners. One afternoon, I was wrestling with another boy in the street when we heard that sinister noise. Suddenly it stopped. We forgot about fighting and looked up. The flying bomb hit a nearby house with a tremendous roar. It was close enough for us to see the glass in the windows of the house we were in front of come out in one piece before they smashed to the ground.

One of our school friends was killed by that V-1, although nobody told us about it officially – he just wasn't there any more. He was a charming boy named Bobby. I had just been given a new chinchilla rabbit, so I called him Bobby in his memory.

When I watched John Boorman's 1987 film *Hope and Glory* about a boy growing up in the war, it reminded me so much of my childhood because it captured the atmosphere and the feelings of small boys in wartime perfectly. We were exactly like the family in the film; by coincidence the boy at the centre of the film, Billy, lived in Rosehill Avenue, so close in name to Rosemary Avenue. Just like in the film, we attempted to live a normal life, and for most of the war we walked through the little park at the end of the road to Martindale Road primary school carrying our gas masks in cardboard boxes. We would often pick up shrapnel. When lessons were interrupted by air raids we would all be herded into long shelters in the sports field. They never attempted to teach us during those raids, so we quite liked it, even though boredom soon set in.

Despite the uncertainty of the world outside, my parents created an atmosphere of tremendous security inside our typical suburban house. The front door opened into a cramped hall with stairs leading to three bedrooms. There were two downstairs reception rooms – the front one and the back room – although we mainly used the back room – and a tiny kitchen. Central heating was unheard of, so it was a question of keeping a couple of rooms warm. Once a week when we had a bath, the water had to be heated in a big copper in the kitchen and taken up to the small bathroom in a bucket.

I had the smallest bedroom – it was just 6ft by 7ft. It is amazing to think that for a time my mother let it to two teachers. How they managed in such a tiny room I can't imagine. Apart from that, no visitors ever seemed to come into the house except for one of my father's friends.

My brother and I inhabited this apparently safe, enclosed world. My parents knew the neighbours but when they met it was in the street, at the shops or over the garden fence. Everyone would be in their gardens during the summer, the men mowing the lawn or kicking a ball about with the children. My mother was friendly to the neighbours, but she kept her distance. The idea of having people to dinner or entertaining the way we do now never entered their heads.

I believe that confidence is the one crucial quality needed for success and our parents gave us so much of it on their limited means that it paved the way for both John and me to succeed. Although we didn't have much money, they channelled a lot of love and energy into us. There was strict food rationing – children were only allowed two ounces of sweets a week – but I cannot ever remember feeling hungry. My mother was a really good cook and she must have held back so that my brother and I had all we wanted. She built her whole life around her two boys, making sure we lived in a light-hearted and relaxed atmosphere.

I cannot ever remember our mother criticising me – and anyone reading my school reports would know she had plenty of reason to. One thing she instilled in us was the importance of generosity. She told us that meanness was the worst thing of all.

But growing up in the shadow of my handsome, talented elder brother was a bugbear. I felt at a constant disadvantage to John. He seemed to be successful at every-thing he touched, while I failed at most things.

John was blessed with good looks and a fine brain. He did well at school and passed his 11-plus. When he was called up, he was given a commission in the Army. He was my mother's blue-eyed boy who looked down on me from lofty heights. By contrast, I was pretty hopeless at school apart from in art and maths. John set the pace and honed my competitive nature that gave me the motivation to create something. He was my benchmark and the one who led the way in our boyhood entrepreneurial adventures. Although I failed my 11-plus, my mother refused to accept that I would go to the local secondary modern school. What she did taught me that you do not have to take people's first offer in life and you don't have to take no for an answer – there is usually scope for negotiation.

My mother went to see someone in the local education authority who reviewed the paper and said that I had only just failed the exam and that I was obviously a bright boy. Somehow I was given a spare place at a grammar school. The problem was that it was an hour's journey away in Ealing – at Drayton Manor Grammar.

Aged 11, I had to travel first on the Tube to Northfields and then by bus. I found myself at a school of 500 boys and girls where I knew no-one. There was a uniform, which I quite liked – the cap had a long peak on it. The school badge was a phoenix in flames.

I am naturally gregarious and I quickly made friends among the livelier, naughty boys. I found them more fun than the goody two shoes and I was fond of a bit of mischief myself. One time I bought a cheap lot of Ex-Lax chocolate and sold it to the other boys pretending it was ordinary chocolate. There was a huge queue for the loo and the finger of suspicion quickly pointed to me. I was in deep trouble.

Small wonder my form mistress's remarks at the end of my first year were as follows: 'Conduct very unsatisfactory. He is lazy, inattentive and exerts himself to prevent his neighbours from working. He could do much better if he were more ambitious.'

Her instincts were spot on, because once ambition set in later there was no stopping me. But no matter how bad my report, my parents never scolded me. It was either 'Oh well, I'm sure you will do better next time,' or they blamed the teachers or the system. Their attitude rubbed off on me. I still try not to judge other people. Accident of birth and sheer luck have so much to do with how we turn out.

* * *

My mother, who was christened Annie but was always called Nancy, was born in 1896 in Chelsea Barracks where her father was an Army tailor. Like my father, she came from a family of nine children which moved around with the Army.

During the war she worked for the Prudential Insurance Company. Instead of the famous 'Man from the Pru' who featured in the advertisements knocking on people's doors to collect premiums, she was 'the Woman from the Pru'. Once the war ended, however, she gave up work and devoted herself to us. She did everything, kept house, made and mended our clothes, and looked after the chickens which occasionally laid eggs.

I was animal mad as a child. I had a variety of pets – mice, hamsters, guinea pigs and rabbits. When I grew up a bit, I was given a bull terrier called Simba, whom I adored. I have had dogs for most of my adult life. The latest are spaniels called Mabel and Grace. My love of animals and the countryside came from my father, who used to cut out a column called 'Nature Notes' from the *Daily Mail*, which he would give to me.

We never had much in the way of holidays the way people do now, but we rarely thought about it because nobody else in Rosemary Avenue had holidays either. I do, however, recall a week in Cromer in Norfolk and another on the Isle of Wight.

Just after the war my mother took charge of her sister's boarding house near Brighton for a few weeks and she took me with her. We would go to the beach in the afternoons and she took the opportunity to fatten me up on hotel portions.

My parents may have had relatively modest means but they were very keen to give us opportunities. They both loved playing tennis and when I was a baby they would take me in the pram to the courts in the local park while they played. So it seemed natural for me to take it up although strangely my brother never really took to it – it was one thing I was better at than him. I like the competitive nature of tennis and I still play most weeks at my local club.

There was great excitement on Saturday mornings when the local children used to go to the Ambassador's cinema opposite the Tube station on Bath Road; it was part of the Odeon group. The interior was decorated lavishly and the seats were red plush. The tension would mount as up from the pit came the music followed by the man playing the Hammond organ. The films playing were mainly Westerns. *The Cisco Kid* was my favourite starring Duncan Renaldo as the Kid and Leo Carrillo as his side-kick Pancho. Afterwards the boys would all pile out on to the street, play-acting riding horses and shooting each other. That sparked my love of horses and I really wanted to learn to ride.

My father found some stables in Englefield Green in Surrey. The stables had been a garage but the war had killed the car business so the owner bought a few horses and started giving lessons. My father and I would cycle the twelve miles to Englefield Green on Sundays. I would clip-clop round the village while he had a pint in the pub and read the newspaper. We didn't do it very often but I learned how to stay on a horse. I later bought a house in Englefield Green where my wife and I spent most of our married life.

After the war I found another riding school behind the Great West Road. People were just starting to go out and enjoy themselves again and the village of Heston decided to throw its first peacetime fete. There was a competition for mounted fancy dress and I was keen to enter. However, because I was relatively new to the stables all the horses had been bagged by the other kids. Undaunted, I found some gypsies on Hounslow Heath and persuaded them to let me hire a big piebald horse. To the neighbours' amazement, I brought it home and kept it overnight in the alleyway between the houses.

On the day of the contest some neighbours dressed me up in some old sheets as Lawrence of Arabia. We met a band of air cadets marching to the fete and tagged on behind with the horse getting quite frisky. We made a big entrance and I won the contest. I think I bought some carrots for the horse with my 5 bob (25p) winnings and spent the rest on sweets.

I have always loved horses and these days I am lucky enough to ride my own, a handsome grey called Ben, at weekends on our farm at Little Compton in Warwickshire. He is a boarder at the local stables during the week where they look after him royally.

Not all my father's efforts on my behalf worked out. He tried hard to interest me in Rugby Union, taking me to matches at Twickenham. He even bought me a rugby ball one Christmas, but I am afraid I never learned to enjoy team games. Research shows that business builders tend to be more interested in individual sports like tennis or squash.

My brother and I scrapped quite a bit when we were little. A four-year age gap does not make for the greatest harmony and I must have annoyed him in the way that younger brothers do. Nor was he very tolerant of me. My father nicknamed him 'Stormy Petrel', which gives you an idea of his temperament. The only time my mother got really angry was when we fought – she would hit our legs with a strap to separate us.

As we grew older, our relationship improved, especially when we started working together. Whenever John had an idea that needed extra labour I fell in as his helper.

John saw the importance of making money well before I did. He had a moment of awakening when our boiler burst one winter. Our parents were devastated because they could not afford a new one. John says he heard them talking and promised himself never to be in a similar position when he grew up.

I mentioned earlier that our first venture was making

lead soldiers. This was towards the end of the war in 1944, when I was 10 and John was 14. He traded a little plastic revolver for a mould of a mounted soldier and we took the lead from the pipes of houses that had been bombed. We boiled up the lead in a huge ladle over the gas ring in the tiny kitchen in Rosemary Avenue and I remember pouring it into the moulds wearing huge heat-proof gloves.

Afterwards we painted the soldiers and sold them through the lady who delivered milk in a horse-drawn cart – the milkman had gone to fight. The soldiers sold amazingly fast because there were just no toys available then.

I loved Nobby, the milk-lady's horse, and when I was a bit older I helped out on the milk round – following in John's footsteps and getting up at 5.30 a.m.; so I was somewhat annoyed when a form teacher wrote on my report that I was lazy. I still have that report from my second year at grammar school. It does not make happy reading. My average mark was 49 per cent, ranging from 80 per cent in arithmetic to 27 per cent in chemistry. The real problem was that I had too much energy and I was easily bored by lessons; I was constantly in trouble for talking in class, not paying attention or diverting the other boys. I was always looking for action, seeking some way to make life exciting. I still am, only now I try to channel my energy into something constructive such as starting a new charity, painting or travelling to new places.

When John left school, my father used his contacts to get him a place on a three-year course at the London School of Printing.

That led to our next venture, customising greetings cards. John got hold of some blank cards with nice pictures on the front, so we would print personalised greetings for Christmas cards. We sold them to friends, neighbours and family; we also sold them door to door. I seem to remember that I pulled the handle of the press to print each one.

Despite my troubles at school, I left aged 16 having passed the school certificate in five subjects with a distinction in maths and a credit in art. My facility for maths came from my mother who had a real head for figures; the artistic ability came from my father. He drew beautifully and I still have one of his pen and ink drawings hanging in my home. Both talents came in handy when it came to opening employment agencies.

I had, however, set my heart set on being a farmer. I had joined the Young Farmers when I was 14. This meant I could go on Harvest Camps, which had been started during the war by the Ministry of Agriculture. The idea was that young people would replace the men killed or injured to help with the harvest. You would be sent to a farm in the countryside where you were provided with accommodation under canvas and your food was paid for. Although the work was hard, I loved it.

In my final year at school my father had put me down for a year's agricultural course but my school certificate marks in science were not good enough for me to get in. I was bitterly disappointed at the time but I am glad about it now because my life would have been very different. I would not have enjoyed running a farm full-time and I would certainly never have made as much money as I did in the recruitment business. I have ended up owning a farm, which I really enjoy, but I am lucky to have Peter Green, an old friend and able farm manager, to run it.

An uncle in South Africa worked for Tozer, Kemsley and Milbourn, a trading house in the City of London specialising in exporting motor vehicles, so I knew the name. One day I just went in and asked for a job and they gave me a junior office boy post. Each day I travelled on the Tube to Bank Station and walked to 84 Fenchurch Street where my duties included addressing envelopes and running round delivering messages as someone had to before the invention of faxes, email or mobile phones.

At the same time, my mother had persuaded me to enrol on a Chartered Secretary's course which I attended four nights a week – so I never had much spare time on my hands. It was an exacting professional course designed for company secretaries and included law and an accounting paper.

After two years at Tozer Kemsley I was called up into the Army. That was in 1952. I was stationed at Tidworth Barracks on Salisbury Plain with not a lot to do. My call-up was delayed by a few months to let me take my Chartered Secretary's exam. Even so, I failed it that first time – I passed it eventually but it took me some years. I have a bad memory, or at least my memory is highly selective. When they were growing up, my children used to tease me about my 'amazing' brain and how I could not remember facts. I think the more logical, knowledge-based left side of my brain must be the size of a peanut, although I have an aptitude for figures. But the creative right side – the money-making side – is nearer the size of a coconut.

That is why university probably wouldn't have suited me. In fact, I am glad I did not go to university. I learned far more from the senior people around me at work than I would have from professors.

I was unsure what to expect from the Army. I certainly saw it as a break and it delayed my having to make any decision about what to do next. I went half dreading it, half looking forward to it. I asked to join the Royal Engineers like my brother and like him I wanted a commission. When I applied for one, I was sent to the War Office Selection Board held at Barton Stacey near Winchester in Hampshire.

They put us through our paces over two or three days. You had to get across a bit of a ditch with a plank that was not long enough and take it in turns to lead a team; I remember there were various discussions. Anyway, I failed – twice. I wanted to know why and was offered the opportunity to see the Brigadier who had been in charge to find out. I remember standing to attention while he flicked over some pages. Then he said: 'Reed. Muddled thinking. That's why you failed: muddled thinking.' So there was no commission for me and yet another reason why I needed to prove myself later on.

My own explanation of the Brigadier's unflattering conclusion was that it was 'different' thinking. They would not want different thinking in the Army, would they? No room for lateral thinking!

It is true, though, that I do not respond very well to external discipline. What is the point of rules for rules' sake or doing something one way just because that is how it has always been done?

* * *

One morning I was summoned to see the commanding officer, who told me that my father had been taken ill and that my brother and his fiancée Jenny were coming to collect me and take me to him. The truth was it was already too late. He had already died of a massive heart attack. He was only 61.

I remember being overwhelmed by grief and I still find it difficult to think about it without tears coming to my eyes. The sense of loss was huge. He used to tell both me and John to 'be a big man' and perhaps that has influenced me in the way I live my life.

My mother was devastated, and one reason I continued to live at home for so long was to keep her company.

I know many people say they found Army discipline useful in shaping their characters but I could not really see the point of marching about on Salisbury Plain – especially as the war was over. The Army clearly took the same view, because we were allowed home most weekends.

That was how I hit on my first solo money-making scheme. Every weekend the troops travelled back to London on coaches from Tidworth to Waterloo. If the driver was friendly, I would even get him to drop me on the Great West Road, close to home. One night everyone was complaining because the bus was late and there was talk about switching from Tidworth Coaches to the rival Wilts & Dorset bus company.

The following morning I rang Tidworth Coaches out of the blue and said, 'Look, I was on your bus last night. All the lads are talking about going on Wilts & Dorset instead. Would you like a rep?'

The owner thought it was a great idea, so I took charge of selling tickets. I was a corporal by that stage and every Thursday I would go to the YMCA canteen, which was slightly more luxurious than the NAAFI, and sell bus tickets. On Friday evenings, when we went home, I would count the boys on. The owner, who also drove one of the coaches, trusted me with a great wad of notes along with his Vauxhall which I would drive home to Hounslow and then return it to him over the weekend. They paid me well and I made more money out of Tidworth Coaches than I did out of the Royal Engineers. The arrangement lasted for the rest of my national service.

I got into one big scrape during my short Army career. For a few weeks I was put in charge of the armoury. If they were leaving the barracks for the weekend, the soldiers would bring their rifles back, clean them with a rag called 'four by two' (because it measured 4in x 2in) and throw the oil-soaked rag in a bin. We all smoked back then and after they had all delivered their rifles I locked up and went to lunch. When I came back, the place was ablaze. I have never been sure whose cigarette started it but I was convinced I would end up in the glasshouse. So I told the officer in charge that I did not smoke and he let me off. An extremely efficient commanding officer had the damage repaired by that evening.

When I came out of the Army I finally managed to pass my Chartered Secretary's exam, which was the entry ticket for anyone who wanted to be a company secretary. Although it took me a long time and I failed it twice, what I learned served me and my companies well. I have always been able to understand quite complicated financial problems, which has paid off handsomely over the years.

I returned to Tozer Kemsley, which offered me a job in South Africa but meanwhile, I had also replied to an advertisement for a trainee accountant to join the American company, Gillette. They had a big modern office in West London and made razors and a growing range of men's and women's toiletry and haircare products. The pay and conditions were above those of most British firms so there were plenty of applicants.

I was in two minds about the South African job, partly because my brother was now married and I did not want to leave my mother alone. The next day she rang me at work to say there was a letter for me. It was from Gillette, asking me to go for an interview. To find the time to attend, I asked my boss at Tozer Kemsley for the day off, telling him I needed to go to South Africa House to do some research.

The interview went so well that I was offered a job on the spot. I had to go back to Tozer Kemsley and confess I had been for an interview and had decided to join Gillette rather than go to South Africa. That decision opened the door to a whole new world.

CHAPTER 2

Business American-style

A FTER THE GLOOMY, old-fashioned offices of Tozer, Kemsley and Milbourn in Fenchurch Street, entering Gillette's airy British headquarters felt like stepping into another era. The factories built along the 'Golden Mile' on the Great West Road symbolised the industrial success of Britain in the first half of the twentieth century. Built in 1925, the road attracted a clutch of American companies including Firestone and Gillette, all vying with each other to put up the most elegant building. Designed by Sir Banister Flight Fletcher, the distinguished English architect, and completed in 1937, the Gillette building at Osterley was famous for its distinctive clock tower, later listed. Inside, the management offices at the front were tastefully decorated and furnished with expensive antiques including Hepplewhite chairs. I shared a spacious office with three senior accountants on the second floor overlooking the Great West Road.

There were also three restaurants for staff. Those of us on monthly salaries lunched in the middle restaurant, where the food was good and also free. The personnel department organised the seating so that everyone sat next to people from a different department to increase our knowledge of the company. Those paid weekly ate in a canteen with the factory staff, while the directors took luncheon in their own exclusive dining room. One thing that impressed me was that the restaurant I went to served not only lunch, but also afternoon tea, where cucumber sandwiches were offered along with 'gateau', which was over the top even then.

I had already passed my driving test as my father had paid one of my friends to teach me. So I bought my first car, a beautiful second-hand beige Austin A40, and drove it proudly into work each day.

I joined Gillette as an accounting trainee, spending time in each department although I seemed to get stuck in 'Wages' for a long time. Luck, however, was on my side. One of the divisions produced the Toni permanent wave kit, marketed to women who could not afford to have their hair permed professionally at a salon. The advertisement showed identical twins with identical wavy hair accompanied by the slogan 'Which twin has the Toni?' The idea was that one was a professional salon perm while the other was done at home with the Toni kit at a fraction of the cost.

The truth was that both were utterly professional. Gillette employed the Mayfair-based celebrity hairdresser 'Raymond' (Pierre Raymondo Bessone), also known as 'Mr Teasy-Weasy', to do the perms before the photo shoots. He would style both twins' hair – the only difference was that with one he used his salon perm lotion and with the other he used the Toni product. He managed to make them look iden-tical – at least for the time it took to shoot the commercial.

This campaign made the Toni home perm a bestseller, but it just so happened that the chief accountant of Toni had been having an affair with a celebrity. Worried that the scandal might leak, the company packed him off to a job in Italy. I was in the right place at the right time and they gave me his job. It was quite a leap up the ranks, so I was very happy.

The difference between working at TKM and Gillette was far more than just location or working environment. The cultures were like night and day. At TKM I mainly had to turn up on time, do what I was asked and keep my nose clean. At Gillette the management encouraged the staff to come up with ideas. They provided an 'ideas box' and if they thought they might use one they gave you a 'tenner', which was worth having in 1958.

When Archie Norman took over the floundering Asda supermarket chain in the early 1990s the press made a big deal of his 'Tell Archie' scheme where 'associates' were asked to tell him their ideas. Gillette was more than 30 years ahead of him.

I used the same approach at Reed. A really good idea that made us money would earn the person who came up with it a bonus. I once gave £100,000 to one of our graduates for an idea that made us number one on the internet, of which more later.

At Gillette I used to push ideas at my bosses, sometimes on a daily basis, and because I was an accountant my schemes were usually financially arcane. For instance, I saved them a lot of money on stamps. At the time every receipt had to be signed over a postage stamp. We had about 20,000 customers at Toni, mainly small pharmacies, and by law each had to be sent a receipt for every order. My idea was to stick the receipt on the back of the cheque because in those days banks returned paid cheques to the drawer, so sooner or later our receipt would make its way back to the customer. That saved Gillette the cost of posting 20,000 envelopes a month.

I also put forward the idea of an electric razor with disposable blades. My bosses dismissed it at the time – they thought it was technically impossible – but 50 years later, Gillette has come up with exactly that. Sometimes you can be too far ahead of the game!

Coming up with ideas for Gillette did not stop me experimenting with my own money-making schemes in my spare time. I knew the sort of toiletries they produced at Gillette and realised that if your turnover was less than £1,000 there was no purchase tax to pay. Purchase tax was then an astonishing 95 per cent. So I decided to become a small-scale aftershave manufacturer.

I tried mixing various ingredients and tested the solution on friends and colleagues until I thought it smelled right. The main ingredient was alcohol. I ordered a large quantity and when it was delivered I put it in the garden shed. A week later there was a knock on the front door; it was an official from Her Majesty's Customs and Excise who wanted to know where I was storing the alcohol. Did I know it had to be stored in a bonded warehouse, he asked. So our garden shed became a bonded warehouse and I brewed the aftershave in my mother's big copper. It was quite a process, but eventually the aftershave was decanted into bottles with a nice label. I called it Caprice.

Most of it I sold door to door, but I also tried to get a local hairdresser to stock it. The owner took one bottle, which to my annoyance sat in his window for weeks. Finally I persuaded one of my friends to go in and buy it, telling the shopkeeper what a fantastic product it was and how he had been looking everywhere for it. A day or so later I went back and sold him three more bottles. I sold quite a bit here and there, but, as far as I remember, nobody ever asked for it a second time.

While I was at Gillette, one of our customers went bust, and we were notified that all the stock was being auctioned. I persuaded my bosses to let me have a day's holiday to attend. It was my first time at an auction, but most of the other potential buyers were seasoned hands, many of them barrow boys. To my annoyance, the first lot of Vosene shampoo went before I had a chance to get my hand up. Next was a lot of Silvikrin, another shampoo. I was determined to get it so I kept putting my hand up until it was knocked down to me. I noticed there was a bit of a rumpus going on and then someone said to me, 'You silly bugger, you know you have paid more than the wholesale price?' I calmed down after that and secured another lot – this time of condoms.

I used my car boot as a temporary warehouse and the following weekend I was in the street chatting to my mother about something when I absent-mindedly opened my car boot and box-loads of condoms cascaded out. She pretended not to notice.

I never liked to be idle or poor so I found another sideline – and another source of income. I had a girlfriend named Anne Watts whose father was an estate agent. He had a double-fronted shop just off Hounslow High Street, on the corner opposite the Hounslow bus garage. Mr Watts was not the world's greatest estate agent, but he was the loveliest chap, if a bit irascible. He took me on part time, paying me a retainer plus a commission on every house we sold – and I also used to find houses for him to sell. I would go there at weekends and most days after work.

After three years at Gillette there were no more promotions on the horizon and I started to get restless. When my brother set up his own printing company called John B. Reed in 1959 I thought, 'Oh, God, I'm going to get left behind again.'

I spent a lot of time at Gillette thinking, 'What the hell can I do to be self-employed?' I felt frustrated – I had so many ideas and no way of putting them into practice. In the end the desire to start my own business was like a disease; it felt as though there was something inside me that had to come out. It was like a boil that had to burst.

It wasn't the prospect of making money that motivated me; I wanted to be in charge of my own destiny and experiment with my own ideas. Although I liked Gillette, I disliked being a small cog in a big machine. Nor did I like the idea of becoming an accountant for life.

Finding good staff was increasingly difficult in the late 1950s and Gillette was constantly taking on new people. As the Toni accountant, I signed a lot of cheques to employment agencies which seemed to be doing very well. That made me think starting a new one might be a good place to begin.

Like Victor Kiam, the man who coined the slogan 'I liked the shaver so much, I bought the company,' I was not the first person to turn from a customer into a supplier.

Mr Watts used only half of his double-fronted shop for the estate agency business. In the other half he sold carpets but it was a deadly slow business. So I asked him if he would consider using that half of his shop to open an employment agency. To my disappointment he turned the idea down.

Two weeks later I came up with another proposal. 'You only sell about one carpet a week for £10 profit, so how about renting that half of the shop to me for £10 a week and I will have a go at starting my own employment agency?' To my delight, he agreed – another example of how you should never take no for an answer.

So on 7 May 1960, in the other half of Mr Watts's shop opposite the bus station, I started Reed Employment. I left Gillette on Friday, 6 May and the following Saturday morning I opened the first ever Reed Employment office. I was 26 and felt so elated and excited that I had no thought of being nervous.

That Saturday the newspapers were full of the marriage of Princess Margaret and Antony Armstrong-Jones, who had set off for their honeymoon in the Caribbean on the Royal Yacht *Britannia*. I was far too busy to think much about that.

Everybody said I was making a big mistake leaving Gillette. My colleagues thought I was taking a huge risk leaving a nice, well-paid job to launch out on my own, but it was what I wanted. I had £75 saved up in the Gillette pension fund – worth a few hundred today – and I was still living at home, so my expenses were small. My mother, although worried, supported me as she always did.

My old colleagues at Gillette were very good to me, asking me to fill several jobs for the company and so I made my first placement. They also helped me furnish the place. Gillette had a sale of old office furniture and I bought a secretary's desk and chair for £1 10s. The desk had a well in it where the typewriter would sit, so one of the handymen made a smooth top for it. I paid him to paint the shop sage green, which became the Reed colour for many years. I would always wear sage green socks to work and we printed the letter heading in the same colour. I had the first fascia made of big metal letters.

I filled the window with job description cards to attract candidates. We were in a perfect position in Hounslow to attract people as they came out of the bus station. I put some tempting advertisements in the local paper. Then I picked up the phone and called a number of local companies, including Gillette. I should add that getting a new phone line in 1960 was an ordeal in itself, but I found a way through.

Business took off. The first Monday I placed two women, a secretary and a copy typist, and by the end of the week five had been taken on. So it went on. No sooner did the candidates walk through the door than I found them jobs, and within the year, through Mr Watts, I very quickly opened a second branch nearby in Feltham. It too did extremely well. It was not until several years later that I realised that it was not my own genius that was the key to my instant success, but being near Heathrow Airport. It was expanding fast in 1960 and had a voracious appetite for staff.

Naively I thought that was just normal, so it was quite a shock when I opened another half dozen offices in different places and they all started to lose money. I opened in Slough, Kingston, Holborn, Fleet Street and Chiswick. Within three years I had ten branches, but only two were profitable.

There were some unexpected twists. One of our early clients was Penguin Books. About that time, D. H. Lawrence's controversial book *Lady Chatterley's Lover* was allowed to be sold for the first time after a much publicised court case. Penguin was rushed off its feet selling *Lady Chatterley's Lover* and took a lot of temps from us so I visited the warehouse to discuss their needs. After our conversation our contact there said I could have any book I liked. So, of course, I chose *Lady Chatterley's Lover*.

Working hours were confined to office hours of 9 a.m. to 6 p.m., Monday to Saturday. Unlike my competitors, I opened on Saturdays so that candidates who already had jobs could be interviewed then. In that first year I spent Sundays longing for the week to start again so that I could get back to my business. That is why I love Mondays.

In those early years my brain worked non-stop on what I would do next. I had decided to charge 25 per cent more than my competitors. I am not sure why, but instinctively I felt the market could bear it. After the first week when I had sent out some invoices, a client's personnel officer stormed into the branch. Frothing with rage about the price, he said he would never use us again. But he did of course, because his company needed people. There was huge demand for staff in the early 1960s and we kept the supply coming. The employment agency industry had twice-yearly price increases. Finding staff through an agency was much cheaper than advertising in newspapers, but even we did not realise that at the time. Intriguingly, none of my competitors ever put up their rates to our level. I expect they felt they could only gain custom by keeping their fees lower.

My operation was different from the start. The

employment agency business in 1960 was run by middle-aged men and women in an old-fashioned style.

The offices of rivals such as Brook Street Bureau (owned by Margery Hurst), Phoenix or Alfred Marks tended to be dark, located on the first and second floor of a building with a sombre atmosphere. The interviewers would be soberly dressed and there was huge emphasis on typing and short-hand speeds but very little on initiative or presentation. Work was a very serious business – and not in a good way.

One competitor compared the employment agency business before I started to Charles Dickens's description in Nicholas Nickleby (reprinted on the opening pages of this book). He may have been exaggerating, but it is true that the established agencies sat in their offices and waited for business to come to them. As the new boy I felt I had no alternative but to go out and get it.

One of the ways to attract business was to make our window displays interesting. I raised the game for presentation, targeting prime high street sites and making sure the window displays were professionally designed and set out.

I am not sure I thought about it that much, but at 26 I was almost half the age of my competitors and once I started employing people as interviewers I took on bright, well turned-out young women. From the start people at Reed had to look smart and be enthusiastic.

Our offices buzzed and generated excitement. I was forever giving the interviewers little incentives to make their job seem interesting. Each week the person who had made the most placements got a reward such as cinema tickets.

The first man to work for me was Tony Jewitt, who replied to an advertisement. Like me, he was a chartered secretary and joined Reed straight from the Royal Artillery, where he had done his national service. Before that he had worked as a trainee for BP. He had not enjoyed the bureaucratic atmosphere of the then government-owned oil giant and wanted something more lively. Eventually, Tony took over running the branches. He understood my style and we worked well together.

Like any newcomer in a mature Industry I had to break away from the established way of doing things and lead the industry in a more exciting, dynamic direction.

Two doors away from our Hounslow office, Fox's the sweetshop closed and the premises were put up to let. We discovered that a competitor had bid for them and so we hopped in and outbid him. We did not want another Reed branch virtually next door so we named it King after some friends. I expect it annoyed him at the time as his name was Brian Kingham. He later sold his employment business to Blue Arrow and went on to found Reliance Security Group.

In the early days we tried a number of approaches to advertising although as the number of branches grew they generated their own publicity. Quite early on we commissioned a young, hot-shot agency run by two brothers, Maurice and Charles Saatchi, to design a newspaper advertisement campaign for us. It was one of their very first campaigns. We allocated £15,000 to the trial and Maurice, Charles and their young colleague Tim Bell, who became Margaret Thatcher's PR guru, all put their creative talents to work.

They came up with clever, jokey ads that went in local newspapers. They emphasised how careful Reed was to match the right skills with the right job – 'Tea ladies do not make good secretaries and vice versa' was one of the lines. Saatchi & Saatchi went on to become incredibly successful, making its name with the 'Labour Isn't Working' campaign that helped the Conservatives back to power in 1979. However, in my view their ads for us were a failure – any impact they made in boosting Reed business was imperceptible.

I was incredibly lucky with my timing as 1960 was the perfect year in which to start an employment agency. We were at the beginning of the most exciting decade of the twentieth century, in which we would see huge social and economic changes in Britain, Europe and America. There would be new music, new clothes, new industries and the expansion of the consumer culture that had begun in the mid-1950s. As Britain struggled out of the immediate post-war era, wages rose dramatically. Between 1961 and 1971, average personal disposable income rose by 20 per cent, from £532 a year to £638. The middle classes did even better with the average earnings of salaried employees rising by 127 per cent between 1955 and 1969. Teenagers began to have money to spend and the arrival of the contraceptive pill – so much more convenient than other forms of birth control – gave freedom to young women who wanted to work and develop careers rather than have children the moment they married.

The new consumerism fuelled the growth of advertising agencies, the music and entertainment industries while advancing technology created more white collar jobs. Manufacturing remained important though there was a shift from heavy engineering to making cars, televisions, washing machines and refrigerators. Alongside all the changes taking place came a wealth of service jobs. Reed Employment, specialising mainly in secretarial and clerical staff, grew fast against the backdrop of the Beatles, Carnaby Street and a new entrepreneurial spirit.

* * *

Once I realised that new branches did not necessarily make a profit from the first day I had to find out why. The main reason was simply location. I also realised that a branch that makes money straight away is a fluke and not, as I thought at first, normal. I now know that a new branch is an investment that needs to be nurtured.

As we grew, I realised that I needed more people. One of my slogans is 'Delegate, Innovate and Energise' – DIE for short. I have never tried to do everything myself. I do like to be in overall control, but once I see that someone is up to the job, I let them get on with it. And I knew I needed some help finding good sites.

The biggest problem – apart from getting telephones into new branches – was persuading local councils to give us 'change of use' planning to turn a retail shop into what they regarded as 'office use'. During the first two years, most of our sites – apart from the first two – were first-floor offices like other employment agencies.

I soon realised that to make an impact and attract both clients and candidates it was far better to be on the ground floor. That meant we came bang up against the local councils. Retail use, or Class A, commanded the highest rents and was regarded as the most desirable by investors and landlords. So there was huge resistance to office use, or

Class B in retail sites, because offices didn't attract as many people and the overall footfall would drop. The argument by councils was that the owners of neighbouring shops would object because rental values would fall.

Someone more conventional might have employed an expert in this field, but I never like to do the conventional thing. So instead I took on someone with no experience of the property world at all. His name is Michael Whittaker, known within Reed as Mike. I met him in 1962 because my brother was looking for a sales rep for his printing business. He asked me to handle the recruitment and I advertised the job in the *Daily Telegraph*. Mike replied to the ad, came to see me and I sent him off to be interviewed by John in Windsor. The interview went well, but John changed his mind and decided that his business was not ready for a full-time sales rep.

Mike and I had hit it off so well at our initial meeting that I decided to see him again. Mike always says that he was bowled over by my 'electric personality'. He liked my enthusiasm although he was somewhat unnerved because I would not keep still and moved about firing questions. I also liked his enthusiasm and I thought he would be good to have in the business. I suggested he join us and have a go at running the Earls Court office. Mike was born and brought up near Lichfield in Staffordshire, but at 22 he had decided London was the place for him.

He agreed to join me, staying at Reed for the next 40 years, although it turned out that running branches was not his forte. He was and is great company. The day he joined we were holding a dinner and dance for the staff and I invited him along. I remember looking up after about half an hour and there he was, playing the piano with the band.

Outgoing and charming though he is, he was no good at managing people, so one day Tony Jewitt asked him if he would like to have a go at finding sites for new branches. Mike leapt at the opportunity. Our City of London sites were not working out that well so we thought we should target the West End. My aim was to have Reed branches in prime positions in main shopping streets. At that time those sites were far from easy to find.

Oxford Street in those days was not so dominated by shopping as it is now. Although the centre near Selfridges and the Marks & Spencer flagship store was heavily retail, it petered out at either end into various commercial premises such as banks and building societies. Mike had become friends with Peter Heard at Churston Heard, the big retail property agents, and thanks to him had already learned about some of the problems encountered with landlords, investors and local councils. One day Mike spotted that there was a ground-floor Alfred Marks branch at the western end of Oxford Street. He watched it closely for several weeks and was intrigued to see that the branch kept taking on more interviewers. Clearly the business was going well.

Mike started looking at the eastern, Tottenham Court Road end and alighted on a weird outlet that took in laundry and sent it away for cleaning with the customers collecting it a couple of days later. It was no. 72 and not that attractive to conventional retailers as there was a big pillar in the middle.

Mike felt that because of the pillar, resistance to granting a change of use might not be that strong. He discovered that the shop was on the market and put in a bid for it. An initial problem was that the Reed financial covenant was not good enough although there was only a mild objection to change of use.

Once Mike alerted me to this problem I guaranteed the covenant and we took the premises. It was enough of a success to show that ground-floor retail sites on well-known streets might be the future.

After Mike's success with that property I asked him to take over the whole business of finding sites, negotiating with landlords and second guessing local councils. He did it with great success, loving the thrill of the chase, tracking down sites with great stealth and then negotiating. He soon became the Reed property director, throwing all his energy into building our prime portfolio of offices. Even Bernard Marks, who ran Alfred Marks after his father died, says ours was the best portfolio of sites in the sector.

Mike was very much a guiding force in the growth of the company. I gave him carte blanche to act on his own because I trusted his judgement. This caused some consternation within the company, but even more among the competition. Their property people usually had to put a proposal before the directors before making a bid and that delayed their decisions. I have had angry letters from other employment agencies asking me if I knew that Mike was acting on his own, which of course I did. The whole point was that he could act much faster than our competitors.

He would often outbid the competition for a plum site but I did not mind paying a high rent as I realised that having a ground-floor office in a prime retail pitch did wonders for the brand, raised the Reed profile and saved us considerable amounts in advertising.

Mike will deny that he ever overpaid for sites, but he

certainly renegotiated the leases. All leases were for 25 years with regular upward rent reviews. To start again from a new base had its attractions both for landlords and their investors. Another ruse was to find a new location for an existing tenant that he wanted to leave a particular site.

He had a rare ability to assess whether a council would give consent to change of use from retail to office on appeal. If the site had been occupied by a shop, then the council was almost certain to turn down the application first time round. He found that by appealing he could often get that first ruling overturned, having meanwhile won the landlord round.

Mike would have himself driven around towns we had targeted so that he could concentrate fully on the properties. He identified several sites that he felt could win planning permission on appeal. Sometimes he would scare the authority into granting permission by quoting what inspectors had said elsewhere in our favour, threatening them with huge costs should they proceed to appeal.

Occasionally he would even commit us to taking a site, which seemed an almost reckless thing to do, get turned down by the local authority and then go to appeal.

By then we had built up an army of experienced barristers and solicitors and we would be willing to face a public enquiry to get a site. Very often the local authorities employed high-powered barristers so we had quite a ding dong. Some we lost and some were not worth the effort. We had to abandon a couple, but usually we were successful. The longest we ever waited while paying the rent but being unable to trade was fourteen months.

Although it was irritating to pay rent on a site we could

not use I saw why it was a risk worth taking. We wanted to be in the best places where we would be the only employment agency. Mike became exceptionally skilled at finding and securing sites in those prime retail spots. He hated to lose a site to a competitor. There is one in Baker Street that he still cannot bear to pass.

We rode the wave of optimism and economic growth like champion surfers. Employment agencies are an almost perfect barometer of the economy and we found our figures were actually a leading indicator. Our business would turn up or down a few months before the trend became clear in the general economy. The press soon latched on to this and I became something of a pundit, forecasting turning points in the economy.

At the end of the 1960s the stock market went a little bit crazy and Reed was booming. Bubbles are not a new phenomenon and the bull market of 1969/70 was a classic example. So we decided to float the company on the London Stock Exchange – something I still say was my biggest mistake. By then, though, I had a wife and a young family to consider.

CHAPTER 3

Wedding bells

I MET MY WIFE, then Adrianne Eyre, through the Young Conservatives. My brother had married a few months after my father died. Although I was still living with her, my mother would never have dreamed of trying to control my social life, and I was always gregarious and had a number of girlfriends. I had joined the Young Conservatives in my early twenties, becoming chairman of the Feltham & Spelthorne Area. As an aspiring young entrepreneur, the Conservatives appeared to me to be the rational party to support, even though my background was a long way from that of the traditional Tory of the time. Most of my fellow members were, like me, grammar school boys from modest backgrounds but with aspirations. It was also a great way to meet girls.

For a young man about town, Hounslow was hardly the best hunting ground, so I, along with some friends, would make forays into the smarter Conservative areas. It happened that a friend and I had gone to a South Kensington Young Conservatives evening where the then editor of the *Evening Standard*, Charles Wintour, had agreed to speak. Wintour was a formidable figure in British journalism and his daughter, Anna, became the much feared and revered editor of American *Vogue* – the model for the main character in the film *The Devil Wears Prada*. After his talk there was a band and some dancing.

By one of those fluke chances, four girls who were renting a flat around the corner from Kensington Square had also decided to attend. One of them caught my eye and I made a note to ask her to dance after the talk. After Wintour had finished speaking and the music started, I looked around for her but she had gone.

Adrianne had decided that she was not going to stand around and wait to be asked to dance – quite typical of her – so she persuaded her flatmates that they should leave. She has since said that she had spotted a good-looking young man but had lost sight of him. Just as they were leaving, one of her friends said she thought the young man was about to ask Adrianne to dance. Why not go back in and pretend she had lost her handbag to give him another chance? When she came back into the room I spotted her straight away so I walked up to her and said, 'Don't look so worried, come and dance.' She still says it was another young man she had noticed, but I reckon it was me all along.

Cupid must have played a part as that evening was the only time Adrianne had ever been to a Young Conservatives function.

After the dancing, I took Adrianne for coffee at La Dolce Vita, an Italian cafe in Knightsbridge, and we started going out regularly. That was November 1960. We became engaged the following June and married in September 1961, less than a year later.

Adrianne tells me I was different from most of the young

men she had met up till then. She found me fun while they had all been rather serious for her taste. She had been to secretarial college at Oxford where her brother was reading classics at Balliol. Her mother, Mary, thought that her brother would keep an eye on her as she was quite sparky. She still is. But she found his intellectual friends rather dull; I was a quite different proposition.

Her mother was not that pleased when it became clear that our relationship was serious. Adrianne's father, Harry Eyre, had died during the war when she was only three years old. Her mother lived in Torquay with her parents and a brother who had become a veterinary surgeon. Adrianne's grandparents looked after kennels and her uncle practised on the same premises – hence her love of dogs, which we soon realised we shared.

One evening when her mother had come up for a few days in London, I decided to take them both to dinner at the French Horn, a well-known hotel with a great restaurant in Sonning, Berkshire. I had been there just once before with the estate agent's daughter, Anne Watts, and had been treated royally by the maître d'. He had greeted me like a long-lost friend, gave us a lovely table and at the end bought us brandies. At one point he asked me how the tigers were. I thought he must mean some people called Mr and Mrs Tiger and so I just went along with him and said they were fine. It was only after I left the restaurant that I realised he had mistaken me for the late John Aspinall, the notorious owner of the Clermont Club. Aspinall loved wild animals and owned Howletts Zoo in Kent, where indeed he kept tigers.

So I thought I would impress my potential mother-in-law with the restaurant, then broach the subject of marriage and ask her permission to ask Adrianne to marry me. On the way there I was driving and they were sitting chatting in the back of the car. Suddenly I heard Adrianne's mother ask in a somewhat acerbic tone: 'Whatever happened to all those nice young men you knew at Oxford?'

That rather put me off bringing up the subject of marriage that evening, particularly as the maître d' showed no sign of recognising me this time. I eventually asked Adrianne's mother for her daughter's hand by writing to her. She may have been sceptical at the beginning, but after Adrianne and I were married, we became great friends.

We married on 16 September at St Mary the Boltons in the heart of Kensington – quite a smart church for a boy from Hounslow. In those days you only had to leave a suitcase at the right address for a few weeks to claim residency and it was close to where Adrianne was flat-sharing. She persuaded her mother not to hold the wedding in Torquay as she wanted to invite our young friends.

We had the reception at Bailey's Hotel opposite Gloucester Road Tube station. It is a lovely old Victorian building with a magnificent sweeping staircase.

I sometimes say that Adrianne fitted perfectly the job specification of being married to me. She is just sufficiently interested in the business that I can tell her about any developments or problems. She is very interested in the arts and she had an art gallery in Windsor for a while. These days she works one day a week at the shop in the Royal Marsden Hospital, where I was treated for cancer.

She has a strong personality and clear views, but she is considerably calmer than me. One of my closest friends calls her the Valium of our marriage. Whenever I get over-excited about new ventures or worried about business she is good at calming me down and helping me to see things in perspective. We were both born under the sign of Aquarius, the water carrier, which supposedly makes us friendly, honest, loyal but independent. I can't argue with that. Of course we have the occasional disagreements but they are soon over. Neither of us enjoy confrontation nor prolonging an argument. I am not really the romantic type but we still enjoy each other's company after 50 years which must say something about our marriage.

Adrianne's support has never been in doubt, but if she feels strongly that I am doing something wrong or against my own interests, she will tell me. I always listen, but I do not always take her advice; sometimes I have regretted it later, as you will see.

Our first son, James, was born in 1963. Richard came along two years later and Alexandra in 1971. Having children has been an amazing adventure and the arrival of all three was fantastically exciting. Nothing prepares you for the seismic shift that happens when you have a child. By the time James was born we had moved from our flat in Richmond to our first house in Englefield Green, the same village where my dad had taken me for riding lessons. My brother John and his wife Jenny also made their family home there.

I have always loved being a dad and now I love spending time with our 11 grandchildren. I got on well with all our children but in different ways. There were six years between Richard and Alex so she was almost treated as an only child when she was younger. We kept an open, hospitable house and I would sometimes ferry Alex and her friends around. I used to embarrass her with my jokes and singing old songs in the car – 'A, you're Adorable, B, you're so Beautiful' – was one of my favourites. Even so, she now says many of her friends wished they had a dad like me! I may have thought about the business most of my waking moments, but I was usually home at a reasonable hour and rarely worked weekends.

CHAPTER 4

New adventures

W E HAD TEN REED OFFICES by the time James was born, and I moved the head office from Earls Court to Bond Street. At around this time, we took on an attractive young lady called Mary Newham, who started our nursing recruitment division. Mary had been teaching primary school children but she had taken a year off and was coming to the end of it. One day she spotted an advertisement in the local paper for someone to work from our Earls Court office and help find clients for a new branch in Slough. She came to see me and I was immediately impressed. She was not only good-looking and stylish, but she also had an engaging personality that I knew would go down well with clients and candidates.

Apparently she thought the job might be good for six months or so and then she would go back to teaching. She stayed for 36 years, creating Reed Health, one of the most important companies in our group and becoming a main board director until she retired in 1998.

Mary had real commitment and with her warmth and intelligence she was extremely good at persuading clients to use Reed rather than the competition; she also knew how to make the candidates feel special and welcome. Her role was to help set up a new branch and find clients in the area. For a while she worked on our marketing side and she so embodied the Reed ethos that we put her picture on a series of Tube posters. She was dressed in a leather jumpsuit as a lookalike Emma Peel, John Steed's glamorous assistant in the 1960s television series *The Avengers*. Mary was a true 'Reed Girl' who loved the recruitment business.

She said that she had been attracted to Reed by the lively atmosphere at the Earls Court branch. 'Everyone seemed so happy and friendly; it was just a really nice place to work,' she once told me. Mary and I, along with some of the other branch staff, used to play tennis every Tuesday evening in Hounslow. Everybody seemed to have a lot in common – probably because they were all recruited by me.

After Mary set up the Slough office she went to Leicester and opened a branch there, and so it went on. The pressure was not intense, but she felt that I was always moving the business on, opening another branch or a new specialist division.

Before Mary arrived I started the first specialist agency, Reed Executive, which specialised in employing qualified accountants as consultants. It was a natural progression because I was an accountant myself and I understood the market; it was profitable almost immediately. I opened Reed Executive first in Kingston, followed by Bond Street and then rolled out branches in cities around the country.

I was delighted until the defections started. The problem was that executive selection was very much a cottage industry that could be easily replicated. All too soon the consultants I hired saw the possibility of making more money from setting up rival agencies.

One such was Brian Hoggett, who took a team and set up Hoggett Bowers with great success; another was Dickie Phillips, who had been my best man when I married Adrianne. He left me and set up Phillips & Carpenter. I was deeply upset and it took quite a few years for us to be friends again. Defections caused me a huge amount of pain and regret in the early days, but I slowly learned to accept them.

As a result, we converted Reed Executive into a multi-branch business and changed the name of the executive selection branches to Reed Accountancy. We continued to use the name Reed Executive as the umbrella name for the group.

Next I could see that the introduction of decimalisation, due in 1971, would create a wave of growing demand for computer programmers. So we started Reed Computing. We were ahead of the pack in moving into accountancy and computing and by the mid-1960s both divisions were leading their fields. In our 1966 profit statement, which we published in the *Financial Times* even though we were still a private company, we said: 'In the year to December 1966 the company has enjoyed substantial growth in its specialised fields of accountants and computer personnel despite a general contraction in the volume of business. Fees for the year amounted to £31,194, double the figure for 1965.' Among the major recruitment consultants, the company had close to 50 per cent of the market for accounting and financial appointments – double that of our nearest competitor. In 2010, adjusted for inflation, those fees would have been worth about £450,000.

Mary was the queen of start-ups. Any new idea I came up with, she turned into reality. Initially, Mary started a specialist nursing agency, which supplied temporary nurses to the National Health Service. She began by using nurses who had families or other commitments and so wanted to work part-time. She developed that business throughout Britain, but the real breakthrough came ten years later when she discovered the overseas market. She started to bring in nurses from Australia, New Zealand and South Africa. They were excellent, really hard-working, very adaptable and happy to go anywhere, whereas British nurses usually wanted jobs near their homes. The overseas nurses worked hard for six months and then would take off for two or three months' travel and then return to nursing. Mary loved working with them. She even started a couple of branches specifically for overseas nurses, and we advertised in newspapers in Australia and New Zealand for nurses to work in Britain.

Mary was keen to sign up as many of these nurses as she could find, but her efforts did not always work out. In the 1960s Australia and New Zealand offered subsidised boat fares to Britons wanting to emigrate. The Australians disparagingly called them '£10 Poms'. The fares on ships returning to Britain would be very cheap and attracted young Australians wanting to work their way round Europe and the UK.

Those ships used to stop in Spain before continuing to England, so I thought it would be a good idea if Mary went to Spain, boarded the boat and signed them up before they arrived in England and fell into the hands of the competition. So off she flew to Spain with all her promotional kit.

Unfortunately, as she climbed up one gangway, the one leading off the ship was crammed with youngsters fed up with life on board and eager to see Europe. They all streamed off and hitch-hiked across Europe before coming to Britain. Poor Mary had nobody to interview. At the time she was really upset, but she soon recovered and managed to enjoy the last three days of the voyage to Southampton on her own.

An interesting spin-off from the nursing agency later saved the clearing banks millions of pounds. After Value Added Tax was introduced in 1973 when Britain joined the European Union, nursing services were zero rated. Traditionally nursing agencies charged VAT only on their margin – or mark up – not on the whole fee. The taxman did not like it and tested the situation with a number of nursing agencies. He lost every time. Derek Beal, our finance director, realised that banking and charity were also zero rated so it was permitted to charge VAT on their margin only. This showed enormous savings to those clients. This lasted for ten years before the exemption was removed.

* * *

I could not resist trying out new sidelines, including an early venture called Club Pass. Two chaps at Oxford had started a company called Clubman's Club in the 1960s. Membership afforded instant entry to 400 clubs in London and some of the larger provincial towns. Some were gambling clubs, others drinking, some cabaret. Back then the law dictated that you could not just walk into a club and join instantly, but the Members' Multiple Club Card got round that. We just copied the idea with one or two twists.

My mother and father
with my brother John
in 1931

My mother aged 66 beside
the Thames at Marlow in
1965

Our family home
at 96 Rosemary
Avenue, in
Hounslow, where
I lived until my
marriage

Me (at left, aged five) with my brother John (aged nine) on the Isle of Wight in 1939

At a Young Farmers' harvest camp in 1950 – I am at the far right, aged 16

Adrianne and me on our wedding day, 16 September 1961, at the reception held at Bailey's Hotel in Gloucester Road, London

My three children, James (aged 15), Richard (aged 13) and Alex (aged 8), in 1979

The first Reed agency, in Kingsley Road, Hounslow, which opened for business on Saturday 7 May 1960. Holloways next door was the estate agency where I worked part-time

The Richmond Employment Agency in the mid 1960s – from Monday to Friday it was run as an employment agency, but on Saturdays the awning folded down and it was transformed into a record shop instead

One of the Medicare chain, in Staines shopping centre in the late 1970s

The Reed stand at an annual conference of the Chartered
Institute of Personnel and Development in the late 1990s

The Jacobean manor house that came with the farm I bought
on the proceeds of the Reed flotation in 1971. The building now
houses the Reed Business School

ISSUE NO.7 1966

Front cover of *Reed Girl* magazine, 1966, featuring Reed stalwart
Mary Newham in her Emma Peel (of *The Avengers*) outfit

Classic examples of the high-profile Reed Employment
advertising campaigns of the late 1980s

The Reed Re-start programme in Holloway Prison, London, was an innovative, not-for-profit programme providing prisoners with rehabilitation, training and work experience

The enthusiastic launch of a new advertising campaign in 1985. Reed were first movers in the provision of specialist recruitment

In order to compete with them – they were busily trying to recruit our members – we offered the club owners themselves life membership, which we publicised in a full-page advertisement in the *Daily Express*. Paul Raymond, the legendary Soho club owner, became a life member and the advertisement featured a picture of him with the approximate wording: 'Paul Raymond, a Life Member of Club Pass, welcomes you to the Raymond Revue Bar.'

Mike and I went round the clubs to persuade the owners or managers to come on board. I vividly recall going to see the washing machine tycoon, John Bloom, who owned the Crazy Horse nightclub just behind Madame Tussauds in Marylebone. We rolled up in my Aston Martin looking the part. But it was a sleazy world and because I was married with a family I wanted to stay anonymous; so we pretended that Mike was the boss and I was his sidekick. John Bloom was quite a character and at one point he said to Mike, 'Sit down and we will talk. Tell Daddy Longlegs to get us some drinks from the bar.' That is the only time I have ever been called Daddy Longlegs. I went off and ordered the drinks, laughing quietly to myself.

I discovered the great advantage of signing people up via banker's order. We would only accept members who agreed to pay their membership by banker's order; once they had signed up they rarely cancelled, so the money kept rolling in. However, although it was both fun and lucrative, it did not really fit with the rest of the company, so we sold that business to Mecca.

A more staid venture was a company called Inter Company Comparisons, or ICC for short, enabling people in similar industries to compare their performance with others in the sector. Tony Jewitt, my first branch manager, was desperate to go to Harvard so I financed him to go on a three-month course. When he came back I put him in charge of ICC and he did very well with it. The idea was to take advantage of a new law that required all companies to register their results each year at Companies House, then based in City Road, just north of Finsbury Square in the City. We sent clerks into Companies House to do the figure work and sold the information by subscription. The first sector we covered was 'boots and shoes'. You received three reports a year for the £25 subscription.

But when we decided to float Reed, the accountants said that if we included ICC, it would reduce the value of the whole group. So I asked Tony if he would like to have Inter Company Comparisons as a present. He was delighted and did very well with it. Robert Maxwell wanted to buy it, but Tony rejected his approach and many years later sold the company to a Swedish group. ICC Information UK, as it is now called, is still thriving and Dun & Bradstreet, the credit monitoring company, bought the Irish subsidiary in 2009.

I always wanted to make Reed a fun place in which to work or to visit for an interview and from what Mary and many others say, I succeeded. To stop complacency or boredom creeping in, I would continually come up with new ideas to make our staff feel involved.

To give the company some esprit de corps we started an in-house magazine called *Reed Girl*. We copied the idea from 'Kelly Girls', but nobody seemed to mind.

In the early years when we had relatively few shops, we spent quite a lot of money on marketing. In 1966, for example, we spent £28,000 (£390,000 in today's money) on a mixture of poster and newspaper ads. Most of the early advertising for *Reed Girl* would now be considered politically incorrect and would break today's employment laws. For example, we automatically specified someone's gender and age range in an ad – it wouldn't have occurred to us not to. In fact, we thought it was necessary. We had slogans such as 'Reed girls get Extra' and the racy ad with Mary Newham dressed in her Emma Peel outfit.

Unlike our competitors I believed that the window displays were very important so we employed a resident artist. She had her own studio in which she would create displays and then adapt them to the branches.

In 1968 we ran an article in *Reed Girl* with the headline 'Reed girls for £1,000-a-year jobs'. Inflation was already on the rampage – in 1960 I had been earning £900 a year at Gillette as an accountant. Employers also increasingly differentiated between the more highly skilled girls and those who could just manage average shorthand and typing. We promoted the idea that Reed girls earned good money and that opened the door to a sophisticated way of living. A Reed girl, we implied, could go anywhere, any time, and could even mingle with film stars.

One article in Reed Girl, headlined 'Who can afford it – lunch at the Chalet', promoted the coffee shop at the Hilton Hotel on Park Lane. It was a popular place for young women to have lunch. 'Any Reed girl can do it any day of the week on a Reed girl's salary naturally,' ran the piece. 'You might find yourself next to Anthony Perkins or George Chakiris. Cosy atmosphere and a good lunch for about 5 shillings [25p].' Both Perkins and Chakiris were famous Hollywood actors.

Like my managers at Gillette, I viewed our staff as a potential pool of ideas to be tapped. *Reed Girl* was the way to do it, so we ran a full page asking for ideas: 'Earn Yourself a Bonus: Suggestion Schemes £5 to £25. Set out your ideas in space below and send to your nearest branch. Ideas are considered once a month by a committee and awards made according to the committee's findings.'

We also incentivised our temps to promote us to their friends with a bonus of £5, which was offered to any 'Reed girl' who introduced another temporary to our staff.

Reed Girl also carried articles on fashion, health and beauty and we even had a slimming club called Reed Slim with suggested menus and regular meetings after work. We had copied the idea from Weight Watchers, but I don't recall there being a problem. It was all about choosing Reed because we had a particular philosophy. Our basic service was very similar to that of the other employment agencies and I had to differentiate to be successful. I made sure the offices were bright, happy places where the candidates felt valued.

Throwing parties at Christmas or to celebrate anniversaries makes people feel appreciated and cheers everyone up. When the company was small I would sweep everyone off to a restaurant, sometimes taking everyone to Paris on the Orient Express.

I started the Reed Founders Club with an inaugural dinner on 17 November 1967. We held it in the Knightsbridge Suite at the Carlton Tower off Sloane Street and it involved lots of mutual backslapping. The menu was delightfully old-fashioned compared with modern restaurant food. It comprised 'Delice de sole Nantua; Caneton à l'orange, pommes croquette, crêpes soufflé Montraille'. Gillian Packard, the jewellery designer, produced a club emblem. I made a speech on behalf of the founders, Dickie Phillips replied, and Tony Jewitt proposed a toast to the 'Ladies'. How times have changed!

Around that time I moved the head office from Kingston to Bond Street and we started entertaining personnel managers aggressively. At first we would take them to lunch in restaurants but I felt that was too public. So I bought a flat in Hill Street off Berkeley Square and found a talented young cook to make lunch.

It was a fabulous flat, which we decorated stylishly with unusual furniture by modern designers to create a talking point. We hosted lunches there almost every day, although I did not go to many of them. The branch managers took turns to play host and of course there would be plenty to eat and drink. That was the era of the long lunch when people used to think nothing of knocking back a couple of gin and tonics beforehand, followed by wine with the meal and a brandy to finish with. The flat was a great investment and we certainly sweated the asset.

I bought the flat personally for £25,000 because the company was financially stretched by opening new branches and funding temporary secretaries – employers were sometimes quite slow at paying their fees. I sold the flat to the company in the 1970s, after we floated, for £65,000, which was the market price at the time although one journalist tried to make a story out of it. He decided to come to our annual meeting and ask a question in front of shareholders but he was a few minutes late. Our annual meetings were so short then that by the time he was coming up the stairs to the room, we were going down on the way out. Mayfair property prices continued to soar and the company eventually sold the flat for a handsome profit. Judging by similar flats today with the lease we had then, it would now be worth at least £3.5 million.

The mid to late 1960s were a happy period for me and my family. Adrianne and I had two spirited little boys, the business was expanding fast with an enthusiastic team and there was an all-pervading air of excitement. At Reed, we were shaking up the industry and fast gaining market share against the background of 'swinging London'. The music of the Beatles and the Rolling Stones permeated even our conventional lives. Opportunities seemed to be everywhere.

Adrianne and I bought a big Victorian house in Englefield Green for £13,550. It had been built by the founder of Budgen's supermarkets, and for the first time in our lives we experienced real affluence. We began taking family foreign holidays to Italy and France and occasionally Adrianne and I would venture to more exotic places such as Sri Lanka. I developed a temporary passion for expensive cars.

We had driven away from our wedding reception in a Wolseley, and soon after I bought a lovely cream Rover from a songwriter. I remember being so impressed by a tray it had for all the tools – not that I ever knew how to use them. After that I had a red Triumph TR4 before moving on to several Aston Martins when they became fashionable – thanks partly to the early James Bond movies. The Aston Martin DB5 appeared in *Goldfinger*, which came out in 1964; the specially modified DB6 featured in later films. Apart from one new one that was a disaster, I used to buy them second hand and I would always try and negotiate the price down.

One day when I was bantering with a car salesman I tossed a coin with him for the price difference. Sadly he won, but it was a valuable lesson that, given the chance, people will take a gamble. Years later I tried the same trick when buying a valuable carpet – and I won that time, walking away with a free carpet.

James loves to tell the story of his and Richard's first ride in an Aston Martin. It was a sunny afternoon in the spring of 1968 and I took them out in my latest second-hand DB5. We were travelling down the A40 when suddenly steam started gushing out of the bonnet. The boys were understandably scared but I pulled over and told them to get out of the car and stand on the pavement. I opened the bonnet and peered in. I am not particularly mechanical but I realised that the radiator had run dry.

I looked at Richard and said: 'Can you manage a pee?' The boys looked bemused, but Richard nodded and I pointed at a place in the engine and said: 'I want you to pee in there.' I lifted him up and got him to pee into the radiator, and then got James to do the same thing. Then I replaced the radiator cap, got the boys back into the car and off we went.

James sometimes recounts this story in company speeches, telling his audience that the incident gives good insight into the way I think. 'What it tells you about my father is that he is imaginative and unconventional as well as very determined to get where he wants to go.'

* * *

A word here about our competition and the history of employment agencies. The earliest form of staff introduction was informal or through the 'hiring fairs' that started in the middle ages. The first formal agencies flourished in Victorian England, introducing domestic staff to households. By strange coincidence our current London house used to be owned by someone who ran such an agency.

The market leader was a Mrs Hunt, who used to place thousands of servants in private homes and her agency grew so big that she used to keep the staff, who came into London from the country, in hostels in a house near her headquarters in the Marylebone Road. Clerks' agencies came next, as chronicled by Dickens in *Nicholas Nickleby*. They employed mainly male clerks. In those days, because work was scarce, those looking for a post paid the agencies to find it for them.

It was not until the typewriter came on the scene at the start of the twentieth century that women office staff started being employed. The staff continued to pay the fee to the agency right up until after the Second World War, when the tables turned and instead of a surplus of people seeking work, there was a shortage of staff. At that point employers began to pay fees for the staff that agencies supplied. It became illegal to charge applicants and many Continental countries such as France and Germany outlawed the employment agency business altogether for a while.

When I opened that first office opposite the bus station in Hounslow, the employment agency business was dominated by Alfred Marks, Brook Street Bureau, and Conduit Bureau.

Margery Hurst, the founder of Brook Street Bureau, was an extraordinary character. As a young woman she had ambitions to go on the stage and trained at the Royal Academy of Dramatic Art. Instead she opened her first employment bureau in 1945 in Brook Street in Mayfair. She quickly realised that supplying office staff rather than domestic servants was the way forward. She built up a sub-stantial branch network, mainly in suburban London and, helped by her drama school training, she became a brilliant publicist. She soon had the press eating out of her hand, leading to a constant flow of adulatory articles.

Alfred Marks had opened his first employment agency in 1919 in a small office in Frith Street, Soho, the heart of the restaurant industry. He had been a trainee hotel manager, but realised that catering staff had nowhere to go to find specialist jobs in the sector. He began by placing temporary waiters for banqueting. His son, my great friend Bernard Marks, carried on the business after his father died tragically in an accidental explosion during the war with the Territorial Army in Richmond Park. Bernard told me that waiters would earn 5s (25p) for a lunch and 7s 6d for a dinner, out of which the agency would take a commission of 6d (2.5p) or 9d respectively.

Alfred Marks started to place permanent staff and the business grew internationally, supplying catering staff in 70 different countries. During the 1950s Bernard saw how Margery Hurst was building Brook Street by supplying office staff and so in 1956 he followed her lead.

In those days, the industry worked from upper-floor offices, which were regarded as more discreet, but in 1960 Bernard opened the first ground-floor shop on the corner of Waterloo Bridge and the Strand. He claims this was the first proper retail site to be made into an employment agency.

We all did fantastically well during the booming 1960s. The demand for people was so strong that Bernard used to joke that as long as a candidate was breathing when she – and it was nearly always she – walked through the door, she could be found a job. The market for temporary staff also rose dramatically during the decade. Bernard Marks, Eric Hurst (Margery's husband), Ben Philips of Conduit Bureau and I used to meet once a quarter for lunch at either the Westbury Hotel or the Connaught, ostensibly to share mutual concerns, but in reality to attempt to dazzle each other with stories about how well we were doing. Those were fun days, but life was about to become a little more serious as one by one we launched our ships on the uncertain waters of the London Stock Exchange.

CHAPTER 5

Going public

A T THE END OF THE 1960s, the lure of a heady bull market was strong and the siren voices of bankers and stockbrokers seductive. Margery Hurst was the first to take the plunge, floating Brook Street Bureau in 1965, and then Bernard followed, taking Alfred Marks public in 1969. Logic seemed to dictate that we should follow that route even though I was not convinced it was the best. In the end, however, events left me with no choice.

Although Reed made good profits throughout the 1960s, cash flow was tight because we were expanding so fast. We needed money to open new branches, which by then I had learned would take about a year to show a profit. By 1969 we had more than 75 branches, but we were running an ever-increasing overdraft, which, to be honest, we used as working capital. We banked with Barclays and in 1969 the manager called me in and said that he felt this really could not go on. He said we had to take measures to reduce our overdraft.

I discussed it with our finance director and we decided to look for additional capital. Our first port of call was the government-backed Industrial and Commercial Finance Corporation (ICFC), which became the venture capital house 3i. Venture capital later became known as private equity, but the term had yet to be coined.

A team from ICFC took a look at the company but for some reason they turned it down. At that time, there was concern about 'people' businesses that had few physical assets. Venture capitalists in those days preferred to invest in some kind of manufacturing rather than service businesses. I was disappointed, but Barclays still insisted we find more capital.

The only alternative was to follow Brook Street Bureau and Alfred Marks to the stock market, something I would regret doing for the next thirty years. I had never been beguiled by the stock market, where the value of investments can rise and fall on a whim of an analyst or some unexpected government action. I have rarely invested in stocks and shares of other companies. I prefer to put my money into my company and farmland.

Intriguingly, one of the directors of ICFC personally bought shares in Reed when we floated and must have made quite a lot of money as he kept them for many years.

So, with little option but to go public, I set about finding a merchant bank to float the company. This was more difficult than it might sound, mainly because I had no contacts in the City. People tell me I am unorthodox in my business approach – I think I am logical.

I was sent a list of merchant banks and brokers by the Issuing Houses Association, all of which were apparently qualified to handle company flotations. But nobody gave us any clues as to which ones were the best. The City of London is a club, even now, and if you are not a member it is hard to get good information. I did talk to some company chairmen who had already floated, but they were not much help. So I wrote to the head of every company on the list, asking how many flotations they had handled over the past few years and whether they would be interested in introducing Reed to the stock market.

The answers fell into the following categories:

a) Not interested for a variety of reasons.
b) Not done any flotations in the period.
c) Not done any flotations in the period but would be happy to handle yours.
d) We have handled flotations in the period but the bare facts could be misleading, come and talk.
e) Full disclosure, we would like to handle this, come and talk.
f) You don't need a merchant bank, you need a broker to handle this.

We explored this last option, but for some reason the brokers we talked to were not interested in handling our flotation on their own. In the end we contacted those in groups (d) and (e), and went to see them.

We got quite close to appointing Joseph Sebag & Co., an eminent stockbroker headed by Sandy Gilmour, an exceptionally charming Old Etonian. Perhaps he was just too charming, but I felt uneasy with him and in the end I opted instead for Tim Frankland at the merchant bank Hill Samuel, and Rowe & Pitman, the Queen's stockbroker, where Denis Milne looked after us.

Even back then, when there was far less regulation than now, a public offering took up vast amounts of management time and energy and I was thoroughly irritated by it. We were originally going to float in 1970, but a mini recession made forecasting difficult so we came to the market on 13 January 1971, less than a month before Britain switched to decimal currency. Hence the shares of 1s were also denominated as 5p.

Because of the delay, we were able to be very confident about the profit forecast of £310,000 for the year to December 1970 compared with £247,000 in 1969. The 1.3 million shares (a third of the company) were offered on a historic price/earnings ratio of 13.1 and a yield of 4.4 per cent, which compared favourably with both Alfred Marks and Brook Street Bureau, our main competitors.

Another hurdle was dealing with the stockbrokers' analysts and the financial press. Our forthcoming stock market debut was greeted favourably by almost every newspaper, including the *Financial Times*, which concluded its comment piece with the following: 'In view of the scheduled expansion programme the short to medium term prospects look reasonably healthy. Given this, the shares merit a modest premium on the offer price p/e ratio of 13.1.'

In the *Daily Telegraph*, the much respected Questor column wrote:

Reed looks competitively priced. Although no employment agency has yet attracted an institutional following, there looks enough to spare in the price to bail out the stags and ensure a premium of 1s or more. Reed operates from 76 branches of which 66 are in or around Greater

London. In addition, it runs a selection consultancy service for accountancy and computer personnel which saw good repeat business. Last year saw 25 new branches opening. Given that it takes a year or so for a new branch to become profitable, this could augur well for future profits. Reed is an issue to stag or tuck away for the day when last year's openings make an impact on profits.

These articles were hardly eulogies, but perfectly acceptable. There was one small piece in the *Sunday Times*, where the unnamed author recommended that investors should sell Brook Street shares to buy Reed. I imagine that would have infuriated Margery and I can only speculate as to whether she picked up the phone to her influential press contacts. All I know is that Patrick Sergeant wrote a damning piece in the *Daily Mail* the day before the issue closed. Unfortunately for us, Sergeant was highly influential with private investors and well in with City institutions. Under the headline 'Reed, learn, but don't digest' he compared us very unfavourably with the quoted market leader Brook Street Bureau, highlighting our cash problems and concluding: 'Some are keen on Reed but I wouldn't touch them – certainly I would not sell Brook Street to buy Reed.'

Mainly due to him, the offer did not go well – some people even rang up and asked for their forms back, although that was not allowed – and it was only just fully subscribed. Afterwards, to my horror, the shares briefly dipped below the offer price of 12s 6d. Looking back, it was a minor hiccup but at the time it felt like a crisis.

I was fortunate to have seasoned City men at both Rowe & Pitman and Hill Samuel alongside. Although a postal strike held the shares back initially, Sergeant was proved spectacularly wrong over time as our shares soared and consistently out-performed both the FT 30 index in its day and later the FTSE 100 index of leading shares. A thousand pounds invested in Reed at the flotation would have been worth £100,000 at the peak.

Before the flotation I held 100 per cent of the company. I gave a third to my children in trust, held on to a third and decided to sell a third in the float – too much in retrospect – for which at the offer price of 12s 6d I received £330,000. If you look at how the business grew and how our shares performed over the next 30 years you would see that I practically gave them away. Having floated with a value of just over £1 million, the quoted company's value peaked in 1987 at more than £150 million and for most of the 1990s it averaged £80 million. I have regretted giving away so much growth ever since although I and my family always held more than 60 per cent. Something in my psyche needed to know that I controlled the ownership of the company.

The best thing that came out of the flotation was our farm at Little Compton, in Warwickshire, which I bought with some of the proceeds in the same year. A country retreat enhanced our lives as a family, enabling me to indulge my passion for riding and for the children to experience rural life at weekends. Originally we camped in the big house – a stunning Jacobean manor – but it was too big for our tastes to be a manageable family home, so we converted a row of gardeners' cottages in which to live.

I turned the manor house into the Reed Business School, which is owned by the Reed Educational Trust and is completely separate from the company. Reed Business School is run with ruthless efficiency by an all-women team led by Stella Shaw and regularly wins awards. As a bonus the manor has the most wonderful gardens, which we occasionally open to the public. The estate has been a continuing source of pleasure, so perhaps I should not complain too much about the float.

That said, although we were clear from our immediate cash problems, I paid a high personal price. I still had financial control but I had lost absolute autonomy and I was accountable to outside shareholders and under scrutiny from commentators. Everything you may have heard about the City's obsession with short-term performance is true. Once you are head of a public company you are expected to perform; you become a metaphorical unpaid greyhound on a racetrack called the stock market.

CHAPTER 6

On the rollercoaster

OUR EARLY LIFE as a public company sped by in a flurry of branch openings and false alarms. We opened 25 new branches in the year to 31 December 1971, taking the total to more than a hundred, and despite torrid economic conditions, we managed a modest 8 per cent rise in pre-tax profits. The postal strike made our lives tough in the first half of the year, in the days before computers or even motorcycle messengers became commonplace. Record unemployment figures followed in the second half of our year. They spooked the government into introducing measures that set inflation racing ahead; but it was good for business because it stimulated demand for jobs.

Helped by the government measures, our profits cruised upwards for three years. At the end of 1972, business had been so buoyant that I was brimming with optimism. 'It is difficult to remember a time when we could look forward to the future with such confidence,' I wrote blithely in the annual report. Profits had jumped by 40 per cent in the year to December, with momentum increasing in the second half. Everything seemed to be going our way. With my head popping with ideas as usual, I started three new ventures. Our drug-store chain, Medicare, was the most important and the following chapter is devoted to it. Then came the formation of Reed Executive Selection, specialising in middle management; lastly, I tried my hand at publishing with a give-away-magazine called *Roundabout*.

I had little inkling that a bunch of newly rich oil sheikhs were planning moves that would turn most Western economies, let alone my world, upside down.

Inflation worked in our favour during most of the 1970s. We were able to increase our fees twice a year in line with the relentless rise in salaries. From the outset, we had charged 25 per cent more than rival agencies, but I introduced a progressive scale, charging a higher fee as the level of salary rose. It was an innovation that benefited not only us at Reed, but also the whole recruitment industry – Bernard Marks has thanked me several times for coming up with the idea! As inflation took off, it pushed up salaries and thus dramatically increased the total revenue of all employment agencies. Even so, recruiting through an employment agency was still cheaper than advertising; for employers it was the only practical solution to finding temporary staff at short notice.

At Reed we began by supplying mainly permanent staff, but gradually employers' attitudes changed. Whereas in the 1960s temps were used only for holiday relief or when people were sick, by the mid to late 1970s they would be employed at times of higher demand or a sudden rush of business. Employers realised that although at first sight temps usually cost more than permanent staff, the overheads of employing permanent workers were far greater.

Temps did not bring with them the extra costs of holiday pay, pensions and healthcare.

When the economy is buoyant, demand for permanent staff is strong, but temps are more in demand in the leaner times as firms trim the permanent head count. The raising of the school leaving age from 15 to 16 in 1972 created a wave of demand for temps, as companies found themselves short of the junior staff who would normally have come on to the jobs market that summer.

My optimism at the end of 1972 looked justified the following year when profits almost doubled to just short of the magic £1 million; turnover more than doubled to top £10 million for the first time. We were forced to restrict dividends in 1973 due to the government's Counter Inflation Act so the company had plenty of money available with which to try out my new ideas.

Roundabout magazine was designed to be given away free to young women at Tube stations. We already had some experience of magazine publishing with *Reed Girl*, but *Roundabout* stepped up the pace. Each week, the editor crammed its pages with fashion and beauty advice, celebrity gossip and at least one article about a charity. Most important of all, it carried many pages of classified advertising, mainly for jobs to be had at Reed Employment. We launched it in October 1973, but the timing was ill-fated, and there was too much competition. Three other free magazines launched on the same day! Although it was a good little magazine, I closed it just four months later in January 1974. By then property and share prices were crashing and Britain was in the grip of the worst recession since the Second World War.

The crash had been triggered by the oil embargo imposed by the Organisation of Oil Exporting Countries (Opec) in protest about US support for Israel in the Yom Kippur War with its Arab neighbours. Shortly afterwards, Opec quadrupled the price of oil to its largely Western consumers. A banking crisis in tandem with a commercial property bust made life desperate for our customers, who slammed on the recruitment brakes and stopped advertising for staff.

In 1975 our profits halved but, buoyed up by our recent success, I felt brave and carried on investing for expansion. We bought our first computer to start our data-processing department, proudly announcing the arrival of a Univac 90/30 mainframe computer, one of Sperry Univac's new generation of then very modern machines.

The banking crisis of 1974 saw National Westminster Bank come close to disaster; in fact, all the banks were having a tough time. That made them all really jumpy about their loans and because we had such an aggressive branch opening plan, we ran a big overdraft.

During 1974 I also pressed ahead with our first foray into international markets by opening a branch in Paris. This experiment lasted slightly longer than *Roundabout*, but by 1976 we cut our losses and withdrew. The way recruitment was conducted then varied dramatically from country to country, and we were not popular in Paris. Possibly we did not understand the French mentality. It took globalisation and the advent of the internet for Reed to expand abroad successfully more than two decades later.

In any case, we were strapped for cash and the economy was struggling. Two years of constant problems and the enormous consumption of management time were enough. We closed the Paris branch.

I have never been afraid of experimenting with ventures as long as the holding company is not threatened. Providing you learn from it, failure is one of the keys to success. Failing also spurs you to do better – it certainly did me.

So we branched out into new divisions. Today we have more than thirty specialist recruitment divisions. Reed Nurse was one of the first. Started by Mary Newham, it was very successful and ultimately became Reed Health. We now have Reed Doctor, Reed Finance, Reed Marketing, Reed Consulting and so on. An early venture, Reed Accountancy, now has about a hundred branches. We drilled down into the various specialist sectors and more recently we moved into niche areas such as recruiting psychiatrists and pilots. All our subsidiaries are called Reed except for Juxon Farming, the company that holds all the farmland.

We steer clear of the very top end of the market, what the industry calls headhunting, although we regularly place people on salaries of £100,000 and more.

I created silos of companies so that if one runs into trouble it does not pollute the others and bring the whole business down. In effect, this is corporate ring fencing. Reed Global is the holding company and nobody is allowed to give guarantees on its behalf; it is sacrosanct. We protect Reed Global because it is the key to everything.

By the second half of 1976, Reed was pulling out of the recession, although profits for the full year fell to a mere £384,000, compared with £1 million just two years previously.

* * *

My family was growing up during the 1970s. Once the head office moved to Windsor, I was usually home early enough to enjoy the children, reading bedtime stories, playing games or singing to them. I enjoy the company of children and they quickly pick that up. The children remember me as a dad who joked a lot and sang songs from old musicals. Many of the numbers came from the old American songbook. Richard remembers me singing 'Luck Be a Lady Tonight' from *Guys and Dolls* and 'Hey Big Spender' from *Sweet Charity* – Shirley Bassey had a hit with it in 1967, so it was probably in my mind at that time. Alex says I never came down the stairs dressed to go out without singing 'How do I look?'

A favourite song, one that my father taught me, was called 'Galloping Dick'. I always assumed it was about Dick Turpin, although it may actually have been about another highwayman of the same era called Galloping Dick Ferguson.

Like my parents had done with me, I introduced my children to tennis and riding, although in a rather grander style. Instead of taking them to the park, we built our own tennis court at our second house in Englefield Green so we could all play together. And they were lucky enough to have their own ponies.

Once I had realised my dream and bought my farm at Little Compton in Warwickshire, the weekends became much more fun. I bought my first horse, and two ponies called Splash and Jaffa. Richard enjoyed riding at first, but he broke his hip badly in a sleep-walking accident when he was

14 and never went back to riding. James loved it, though, and we took to riding together on Saturday mornings. We used to talk things through on those rides and some people said, as James grew older, that most of the decisions about the business were made on those Saturday outings. Alex also loved the ponies and became a very competent rider.

Unlike me, the children all had formal music lessons and they all came skiing with us, although none of them really took to it. I managed to break my ankle on our first skiing trip and then I broke the other one twenty years later. That was the end of skiing for me – a broken bone puts you 'off games' for too long.

I had wanted to own a farm ever since joining the Young Farmers as a boy. Now, just twelve years after opening my first Reed branch, I had realised my dream. I made the most of it. I employed a farm manager to organise most of the work, but we all pitched in. James and Richard used to help pile the bales of straw at harvest time and set fire to the stubble, which was legal in those days. Once they set fire to a hedge in their enthusiasm.

When I bought the farm, the 350 acres were mainly pasture for grazing sheep. That proved a steep learning curve – I didn't know how hard sheep could kick. We were advised to turn most of the land over to arable crops, wheat and rapeseed, but we also kept some cattle for a while. I remember getting really involved, even delivering a calf by hand – one of my long-held ambitions. James came and watched. He was about 12 then and I know it impressed him because he still talks about it.

Adrianne and I were in our late thirties when we bought Little Compton. We had a beautiful house and lots of friends, so it seemed natural to us to share our good fortune. We threw lots of parties in the Manor. For my fortieth birthday in February 1974 I organised a party for 150 friends. We made it a weekend event and invited some guests to camp in the grounds. I fear it got a little wild on the Saturday night. James, who was looking after the younger children, decided then to make it his benchmark for his own parties when he grew up.

For the Queen's Silver Jubilee in 1977, Adrianne and I joined a big parade that was organised by the people of Windsor, who naturally threw themselves into the celebrations. We paraded through Windsor dressed up as King Arthur and Queen Guinevere. We were followed by other Kings and Queens of England. All the kings had big papier-mâché heads depicting their characters, but the queens were spared and just wore crowns and elaborate period dresses. Our appearance at the Windsor parade was so successful that some nearby villages asked us to theirs in subsequent weekends, so we were quite busy.

On the night of the jubilee several beacons were lit on high points across the Cotswolds – it was an amazing sight, and during the jubilee celebrations Reed branches held plenty of parties and decorated their offices.

At the time, I was also a member of the Englefield Green Golfing Society – EGGS for short – for a while. My brother John loves the game and is much better at it than I ever was – he still plays at Wentworth. Although I am a reasonable tennis player, I never got on with golf. I tired of losing that tiny little ball in the rough, and as I never seemed to get any better, I decided to hang up my clubs.

Another of my passions during the 1970s was carriage

driving. I remember spending a lot of time restoring an old American buggy I bought at the Reading sales. I found the work both soothing and rewarding. One year we entered the Windsor Horse Show; I took Adrianne with me and I doffed my hat to the Queen as we drove past.

I bought a special buggy called a Governess Cart that we used for driving around the Warwickshire lanes. In a way, I was living the childhood I had always wanted and, of course, it was great for my own children. From the start, I established a tradition that we would all spend the month of August at Little Compton. We travelled to many far-flung places during the rest of the year – we went to South Africa twice when the children were growing up – but August is the month when we are 'home on the farm'.

Once we had converted the three gardeners' cottages into our family home, we soon took to spending Christmas there as well. John, his wife Jenny and their three children would come to us with our good friend Rosemary Heywood and her four children. Her husband had left when her children were quite young, so it was good for them to come to us. Adrianne and I are godparents to two of them.

I started one or two other traditions then. Every Christmas I would buy Alex a dress from Harrods. Then I decided I would give the ladies presents on Christmas Eve and the men presents on Christmas morning. I organised lighting the fires and preparing the wine as well as a 'chores' tombola. After Christmas lunch we played charades and other games.

I hated the thought that anyone would feel left out. A neighbour called Mrs Pond lived on her own, so we invited her to Christmas lunch, but she said she preferred to stay at home. Instead, I would send Alex to her cottage with a plate of turkey and all the trimmings and some Christmas pudding.

One year I tested people's sense of humour. I asked three of my friends to dress up as Father Christmas and to come into the hall of the Manor when I rang a bell. They all entered from different sides of the hall. I had not told them about each other, so when they came in they were a bit shocked – they were mirror images of each other. The younger children were totally nonplussed as well, although the older ones thought it very funny.

Adrianne found these big Christmases quite a strain, so once in a while we would go abroad and let a hotel organise everything.

The really big difference between my childhood and that of my children was their excellent private education. The boys went to Scaitcliffe, an unusual little prep school in Englefield Green. It had a long tradition. Alumni include the poet Alfred Lord Tennyson and, more recently, quite a few eccentrics who have done well. Richard Branson is the most famous, and James Palumbo, the founder of the Ministry of Sound nightclub, is another. He was there the same time as James.

Despite being a private school, Scaitcliffe was easy-going, so when James went to St Paul's at 13 he found it a big culture shock. When someone recently asked him if he had enjoyed it he retorted: 'No. Do you know anyone who has?'

Actually we nearly prevented him from going to St Paul's. In those days parents were supposed to apply to only one school for their children, but I have always believed in putting things out to tender. So we put him down for both

Westminster and St Paul's – then deadly rivals, as they still are. The Westminster exam came first and James was offered a place. But it was withdrawn when the head discovered he was also sitting for St Paul's. He was very annoyed, but he missed out on a star pupil. James says it was typical of me not to play by the rules.

Richard also went to St Paul's – and also found it tough going – and then to Southampton University where he read law and achieved a 2.1. The boys are very different from each other – Richard has always been less ambitious than James.

Alexandra, who was six years younger than Richard, went to Cheltenham Ladies' College and read anthropology at Cambridge University before going to Manchester to take her masters in documentary film-making.

James may have found St Paul's demanding, but he did well enough to get into Oxford and subsequently Harvard. I am very proud of them all, but I know university would not have suited me. I just do not have the kind of brain that takes in information and detail that is not relevant to what I am doing. Even so, James says I encouraged him to go to Oxford from an early age. I felt that the times were different, and if my son had the opportunity to go to the best university in the land then he should go for it.

Adrianne and I split our parenting roles quite conventionally. I brought in the money and did fun things with the children after school and at weekends – but unlike many men of that era I did change their nappies occasionally. Adrianne did everything else. She is highly organised and lovingly kept us all in excellent order. Thank goodness, because I have never mastered the art of cooking.

Meanwhile, Adrianne continued to develop my tastes. I had enjoyed musicals since my teens, when my parents took us to the Palace Theatre to see *Zip Goes a Million*, starring George Formby. We had dinner beforehand, one of the rare meals out I remember as a child. But my real epiphany came when a girlfriend took me to the Theatre Royal, Drury Lane, to see *My Fair Lady*, starring Julie Andrews. It was my first exposure to a really high-class production of a musical in the heart of the West End. I was transported.

I enjoyed that production so much that I made a point of seeing any musical that came to town. I also loved the old American film versions of musicals such as *Oklahoma!*, *South Pacific* and *Guys and Dolls*. I have a big collection which I used to watch on Sundays with Alex on my knee – heaven! Even today I like to revisit those old films occasionally.

Adrianne's mother made her a Friend of the Royal Opera House in the mid 1970s, so from then on I escorted her to Covent Garden regularly. On my first visit I saw *Swan Lake*, which had a similar effect on me to *My Fair Lady*. I was hooked. I find that ballet frees my mind in a way that opera does not.

By 1979 the boys were pretty self-sufficient, and Adrianne, who has always been energetic and well organised, felt she had too much time on her hands. Although Alex was eight and took up some of her time, it was clear she needed some focus, so we discussed what she would like to do.

She had always loved art, visiting galleries with friends and she had even taken a few art courses. We were Friends of the Royal Academy and she had got to know some of the academicians such as Ken Howard, Brian Plummer and Charles McCall. After some thought, she said the only thing she was really interested in was art, so I suggested she should start a gallery. Well-heeled Windsor close by seemed the obvious place.

She liked the idea and soon found attractive premises with big picture windows on to the lower part of Windsor High Street opposite the castle. She called it the Compton Gallery, and whatever she put in the window attracted attention.

At that time, the Royal Academy was selling paintings that had not been bought in the Summer Exhibition, so she was able to take her pick. She also topped up with paintings from people she knew on a sale-or-return basis.

The gallery flourished to begin with, but Adrianne's main problem was persuading up-and-coming artists to sell their work through her, before the London galleries discovered them. Naturally, most artists would rather have their pictures hanging in a Cork Street gallery than in Windsor and inevitably she lost some of them to London dealers. She did, however, do a good trade in views of Windsor.

Sadly, the gallery soon became mired in the same early-1980s recession that almost brought Reed to its knees. Financially, it always made a small profit, but I know Adrianne found it quite stressful when nobody was buying. As a working mother with the added complication of dogs at home, she had to juggle quite a few responsibilities. For instance, after she collected Alex from school, she would take her back to the gallery to do her homework. Alex liked that, but it was not ideal. Adrianne knew that if she wanted to really make the gallery work she needed to give it more time.

Sometimes she would hold Sunday private views, which were very successful in terms of selling pictures, but it meant no weekend in the country! Looking after the family meant it was not possible to do it very often. Luckily, she found Michael and Ann Shemilt, who ran the Century Gallery at Henley, and they took over her gallery in 1986.

After that Adrianne still felt she needed something else to occupy her. By that time I had become chairman of the charity Mind, in Egham, and was involved with Andrews, the furnishing and estate agent business founded by philanthropist Cecil Jackson-Cole (about whom more in Chapter 9). It struck me that charities would benefit if there was a central register of potential trustees willing to do pro bono work. Selection of trustees was rather pot luck, based on asking around, rather than any structured approach, so Adrianne decided to compile a register, and she did a really good job. She got in touch with professional magazines such as *Accountancy Age* and the *British Medical Journal*, placing advertisements as well as recruiting by word of mouth. That lasted for ten years until we moved back to London. Nowadays she works one day a week at the Royal Marsden Hospital in Kensington – even in the holidays – and generally organises our busy social life and foreign trips.

By 1977 Reed was booming again, making record profits of £1.1 million. We continued to open new employment agencies as well as four new Medicare drug stores. This took place against a background of industrial unrest, with a long strike at British Leyland, increasing inflation and the continued threat of IRA bombs in Britain. In 1975 a bomb exploded in Oxford Street, damaging our branch there. Since then four more bombs have exploded near our branches, the downside, Mike Whittaker would say, of being in the best positions.

In January 1976 inflation in Britain had peaked at more than 23 per cent, but it continued at around 15 per cent for most of 1977, which meant that rates of pay went up, and along with them our charges.

In 1978, another good year, we tried our hand at the travel agency business, opening our first branch in Moorgate and a second shortly afterwards in Harrow. They both did extremely well and exceeded my expectations. But they didn't fit into the group so we sold them. We also experimented with a scheme called 'Dial a Job' which Patience Wheatcroft wrote about in the *Sunday Times*. We got together a hundred or so employment agencies in the scheme, which actually worked very well in the UK until it was eclipsed by the internet, but it failed completely when we tried it in the United States. I was reluctant to leave the family business at home for very long, so I sent Mike Whittaker to New York to see if he could set it up there, but the agencies and the big employers he talked to resisted the idea.

Eventually a personnel officer in a potential client company told him the truth. Discrimination legislation was then much tighter in the US than in Britain. It was illegal to say you did not want someone because he or she was Hispanic, Afro-Caribbean, female or whatever. As a result, companies had 'friendly' agreements with one or two agencies who tacitly agreed not to send too many candidates from one category. So to have a system where agencies sent out job details to candidates irrespective of race or gender would have spoiled these cosy arrangements. After two months a chastened Mike came home although, being a jazz lover, he had made the most of the New York music scene.

In 1979 Margaret Thatcher's Conservative Party swept to power, and Reed more than doubled its profits to a record of £3.1 million on turnover of £32 million. Our shares began dramatically to outperform the FTSE 100 index, which was hit first by all the economic woes that followed. We did well during the early Thatcher period. The industrial unrest provided opportunities for us – one reason socialist regimes do not like employment agencies – while inflation enabled us to charge more. Ever the optimist, though, I failed to see the forthcoming turn of events.

Buoyed by success, I introduced a shareholding scheme for all staff who had worked for us for more than three years. In order to focus all the shareholders' minds, I put a little test at the back of the 1979 accounts and, as a joke, put 'Time: 5 minutes'. Some of the questions were pretty simple, such as: 'Reed Employment's fees are paid by a) the applicant; b) the government; c) the employer?' But I also included a few more sophisticated questions such as: 'How do we treat the profit on freehold land? a) pay it out as a dividend; b) transfer it to the share premium account; c) transfer it to the non-distributable reserve.' We gave the answers on another page. It was my way of saying that if you hold shares in a company or work for it, you should understand something of how it operates.

CHAPTER 7

Medicare

OR THE FIRST ELEVEN YEARS when we were a private company, I had developed Reed pretty much as my fancy took me. If I thought a magazine was a good idea, then I started one; if an idea failed to work out, then I cut my losses and went on to the next thing. Now, along with a quoted share price I had to face the scrutiny of shareholders, stock market analysts and the financial press, all of whom wanted continued growth year in year out.

Our biggest problem was that the general employment agency business waxes and wanes almost exactly in line with the overall economy. In the good times our profits soared, but in recessions we plunged into loss. The nursing agency was more stable than the rest of the business but it was not big enough to help us buck the cycle.

Our main way of coping with the downturns was to rein back, close branches and stop recruiting staff until better times came along. In a private company this is painful but bearable, but once the company has a share price that rises and falls with the company's fortunes the management is expected to find a magic way of evening out those peaks and troughs.

Faced with this, in 1973 we decided to diversify into retailing. The reasoning behind this was straightforward – we had expertise at acquiring good retail sites and also experience at running branches.

We took quite a close look at copying the high street fashion chain Martin Ford Separates, but I realised that a huge amount would depend on the buyers we employed to choose the stock. If they, a relatively small group of people, got it wrong one season or if only some of them got it wrong or the best ones were headhunted, it could wreck the whole group. I did not like the idea of a business being so dependent on such a small group. Fashion is a tricky area, and I decided against it. In the end I went into another sector I did not fully understand.

Of the various other areas we considered, the one that seemed most resilient to economic peaks and troughs was chemists or drug stores. At the time Superdrug was emerging as a force on the high street with brightly lit, attractive shops which also undercut Boots on price. It struck me as a good business model to copy. There were also quite a few Asian drug stores. You would go through a suburban shopping parade and find everything closed except for a little Asian pharmacy. I believed – naïvely as it turned out – that it would be easy to control stock because the products were all relatively low-priced items such as toothpaste, deodorant and so on. I forgot that they are also relatively easy to steal.

A lot of stock just melted away – a phenomenon known as 'shrinkage' in the trade. Quite early on we discovered that the main culprits were not light-fingered members of the public but some of the staff themselves. I remember visiting the West Ealing shop quite late in the evening just as it was closing. I had wandered in unannounced and watched as four or five of our young ladies sauntered down the aisle filling their shop bags with make-up items; it was clear they had no intention of ringing up a sale on the tills. We tightened up after that, but it was impossible to stop pilfering altogether.

Initially, we went for predominantly working-class areas where we felt basic sales would be constant. Even before we decided on drug stores we had already acquired three London sites – in Tooting, Dalston and Peckham – without knowing what we would do with them. They may have been in poor areas but they were all good shops.

Next we needed someone to run them. We found a chap in his mid-twenties called Philip Hanbury running a little drug store in Peckham. I liked him and he knew the business, so we bought him out and asked him to be the managing director of Medicare. He was good, but I don't think he enjoyed working for somebody else, and after 18 months he left to take a Prontaprint franchise.

We chose the name Medicare because it had the right ring to it – it sounded more upmarket than Superdrug and we felt that property developers, the potential landlords, would prefer it. Our estate agent, David Pulford, came up with the name. We were so parochial in those days that we had no idea that it was the name of the American national medical insurance scheme, which caused some confusion as we grew bigger.

Meanwhile we struggled to manage the business and eventually recruited Tony Burke, who had been managing a Sainsbury's store opposite our Dalston Medicare shop.

Our shop had been having a tough time so I popped into the Sainsbury's to see how they were doing and if they were taking our trade away. The store was heaving with customers so I tracked down Tony who impressed me because he was incredibly knowledgeable about retailing. I managed to lure him away by offering him the job of sales manager and later the managing directorship of the Medicare chain.

Fate was not on his or our side, however. Tony had a company medical when he joined and seemed as fit as a fiddle. Yet a few months later he was diagnosed with cancer and within 18 months he was dead. Sadly, this seemed to be a trend at Medicare – the young wives of two other directors developed cancer and died. As a result I found I was almost single-handedly running Medicare as well as overseeing Reed.

Despite these problems, Medicare was successful at generating cash flow, but for most of the time it made pre-tax losses. However, during the 1970s the government gave stock relief and investment allowances on all new shops. We added several new shops each year so there was also tax relief on the losses. So while Medicare made pre-tax losses that we could offset against the profits of the main Reed business, it actually made profits after tax every year.

The pre-tax loss, however, was a constant talking point at home, so much so that my son Richard even wrote an essay at school about it when he was 13. It started like this: 'Medicare drug store was finding itself making a loss each week. I questioned my father about the chain of retailers but all he could say was that "it is doing better but still making a loss".' This developed into a family joke, because whenever I mentioned Medicare he always responded, 'It is doing better but still making a loss.'

In 1984, after 11 years, Medicare finally made a pre-tax profit and there was much celebrating, but because the company was so badly affected by illness, I found I was forced to work round the clock for some years. Adrianne firmly believed that the stress and worry of that time contributed towards my own colon cancer, which was diagnosed in 1986 when I was 52. Adrianne was unequivocal: Medicare had to be sold.

By then we had 50 Medicare shops. City analysts had never really understood why we had started the business, particularly as it had made pre-tax losses for so long.

So we asked Tim Frankland at Hill Samuel to sell the business. Rather than have a free-for-all auction, he asked for sealed bids. According to my calculations, and those of other drug store operators, Medicare was worth about £10 million. We received three bids at around that level, one from a company called Share, another from the Midlands' Tip Top group and the third from Superdrug. But there was also a fourth bid from Dee Corporation, which became Gateway and later Somerfield, a mish-mash of store groups. Much to our amazement and delight the Dee bid came in at £20 million. Dee's offer was either in shares or cash and the price valued us on a sky-high exit price/earnings ratio of 58.3.

The head of Dee was Alec Monk, who was briefly feted in the City while he built up the company through a series of fast-moving and expensive acquisitions. History shows that he overpaid for most things. The group was later taken private against Monk's will, but the debt he built up crucified it. Medicare was a perfect example of this ten-dency to overpay, and Gateway, as it was then, sold it four years later to Superdrug for just £5 million, having added a further 20 stores. Dee's management had hoped to turn some of their high street sites into Medicare shops, but as most of them were 'off pitch' they did not succeed. Super-drug still has most of our original sites, as Mike Whittaker is always keen to point out, but not the Medicare sites that Dee opened after it acquired the business.

Dee's misjudgement, however, was our good fortune and, as it has turned out, good fortune for many people round the world. As the major shareholder in Reed, my share of that £20 million was £5 million. I was six months the other side of colon cancer, I had no real need of the money and perhaps most important of all, I was not keen to give 40 per cent of it to the government in Capital Gains Tax.

I thought hard about what to do with that £5 million. Apart from my early affection for Aston Martins I have never wanted 'boys' toys' such as yachts, private jets or huge houses. My salary and dividends easily covered our living costs and I certainly did not want shares in Dee Cor-poration. That judgement was spot on, because a few years later Dee collapsed. So I used my £5 million to start the Reed Foundation, directing the money into causes that interest me. I have founded seven charities in all and been actively involved in another four. Encouraging philanthropy is my main mission now; but without entrepreneurialism to make the money, there would be no philanthropy.

CHAPTER 8

Giving it away

I AM NOT SURE IF WEALTH CREATORS are born or made – probably a bit of both. I certainly inherited qualities from my parents as well as learning a lot from them. Above all, they gave me confidence so that when opportunity came along I managed to grasp it with both hands.

Those of us who have made serious money have had a lot of luck. Luck to give us money-making ideas; luck to give us energy and a sense of purpose; and luck to put the right people in the right places to help us along the way.

True, we have worked hard, had good ideas and the tenacity to follow them through. We have been persistent and determined to overcome adversity. But many people work hard all their lives and because of their choices and their fear of taking risks do not achieve much more than the ability to keep themselves and their families in shelter, food and clothing.

Entrepreneurs are vital to the economic health of any nation. When they make money they pay taxes, the people they employ pay taxes, and so everyone benefits. But for me there comes a point of what I call financial obesity, which is bad for anyone's emotional health. Many seriously rich people are seriously miserable!

My solution has been to give away some of those excess pounds to those who have been unlucky or foolish or both. I see it as evening up the way the dice have rolled and broadening my own life. I started my first charity, the Addicts Rehabilitation Charity, to help drug addicts find jobs in the early 1970s. I had set up a small charity in Windsor in 1972 called Reed Charity, which gave small sums to local fetes, hospitals and that kind of thing. I liked to be involved with local affairs and local people. In 1987 I injected the £5 million from Medicare into it, renaming it the Reed Foundation. Then I was ready to go.

In 1989 I kick started both Ethiopiaid and Womankind Worldwide, giving them each £1 million. I also set up Women at Risk in the UK which we later merged with Womankind. The Reed Educational Trust was set up in 1971 as the owner of the Reed Business School.

These days I try to encourage rich people to give away their money intelligently. In 2007 I started The Big Give, an internet charity to help wealthy people unsure of how or where to give. There are more than 7,000 charities listed on the Big Give website, and to make giving more exciting I have introduced 'matched funding and 'challenged matched funding' and geared funding, which can double your donation or even multiply it four times in some cases.

Along the way I rescued War on Want from bankruptcy, served on the boards of Oxfam and Mind and sorted out some problems at Helpage International, part of Help the Aged, now called Age Concern.

Being in a position to help others has widened my

horizons and made my life more satisfying. I have enjoyed using my entrepreneurial skills in setting up charities and watching them grow.

My first experience of the vagaries of how the dice roll came when I was at Drayton Manor grammar school. One of my best friends was always in trouble. He was bright and great fun, but his behaviour was such that he ended up in borstal. We were quite similar in many ways – indeed some psychologists say there is not much difference between the criminal mind and the mind of the entrepreneur. This boy was a good person, but he had a bad start to which parents and school both contributed. It made me realise how lucky I was to have such supportive parents.

So I have always been conscious of those who slip through the net in society – and I have been drawn to help them. The 1960s may have been a boom period, but poverty persisted. In 1966 the BBC TV drama *Cathy Come Home*, watched by 12 million viewers, about the plight of a home-less woman and her child who had fallen through the net of social care, turned the spotlight on Britain's social problems.

In the early 1960s there was a series of articles in the *Observer* about the growing social problems in Britain. Some ill-considered decisions did more harm than good. Moving people out of terraced housing with little sanitation into tower blocks with all mod cons appeared to be improving their lives, but the policy broke up communities and created soulless concrete jungles. People felt isolated and petty crim-inals thrived.

The marijuana-smoking peace and love move-ment of the mid-1960s was soon infiltrated by an uglier drug culture. Although 'peace 'n' love' was still around,

amphetamines and other hard drugs became more preva-
lent, in particular heroin, the most physically addictive of
all drugs. This fuelled crime as addicts needed money to
pay for their habit.

The *Observer* articles described a whole spectrum of
problems, but also gave some practical advice to readers
who wanted to help but did not know how to. It listed charities, their addresses and phone numbers and encouraged
readers to get in touch. It sowed the seeds of an idea I would
adapt to the internet 35 years later with The Big Give.

I noticed in the *Observer* list that there was a centre for
drug addicts near my Bond Street office, so I rang up and
went along to help. It was a matter of convenience more
than anything. I became a volunteer, supervising every
Thursday evening; there was nothing very sophisticated
about it. The idea was really just to keep the addicts safe for
a few hours and talk to them.

The worst part was that there was no provision for overnight care, so at 11 p.m. in deepest midwinter I had to throw
them out into the street. The authorities eventually closed
the centre because it was a fire risk, but a group of us would
take soup to where the addicts gathered just behind Piccadilly Circus.

I wanted to be of more practical use as well. Through
talking to them, I realised that although the addict's first
desire is for heroin, the second is for a job, even if it is only to
earn the money to buy more heroin. So in the early 1970s
I started the Addicts Rehabilitation Charity, which created
the Area Addicts for Rehabilitation Employment Agency, an
employment agency specifically aimed at addicts. We would
find sponsors for each addict – a clean and sober 'twin' who

would provide the personal encouragement necessary to keep addicts employable.

For most of the time the agency worked well. Some people dropped out, but there were also rewarding cases. Years later, while travelling in northern Thailand, I met one of my former 'twins', Alan Cooper, in Chiang Mai, where he had become a monk. It might not have been the life I would have chosen but it was so much better than being a heroin addict and living on the street. Another time I met the daughter of a man called Michael whom we employed through the agency. That job had proved a stepping stone to a good career and drug-free life. She told me how her father had talked about the help we had given him, saying we had saved his life.

I ran the agency for four years until Nick Fenton, who was managing it, told me that there was such a desperate shortage of employable people that there was no longer any need for a specialist agency. So we closed it, and Nick went on to work for Centrepoint, now a well-known charity which houses, supports and educates homeless young people.

Through working with addicts, I met the remark-able David Horne who ran a commune in Chiswick where addicts could stay while they tried to stay clean and get well. He was an amazing character with a long beard and a tough physique – so tough that he used to swim across the Thames at Chiswick to get to the school where he taught during the day. He persuaded me to buy a farm in Corn-wall where addicts could spend some time recovering, and I would occasionally take the children there. I am not sure how many addicts got well permanently, but it was a lovely place and certainly provided pleasant respite for them.

My desire to help others at that time was partly prompted by my new-found Christianity. Neither of my parents had been religious, but I was drawn towards Christianity in my early twenties and was confirmed when I was 28. While working with drug addicts I came across Sandy Miller, a leading criminal barrister, who went on to become the Reverend Sandy Miller, a pivotal figure in the evangelical Christian movement in Britain. He became vicar of Holy Trinity Brompton, attracting a huge following. He was the main founder of the Alpha Course, which recruits people into Christianity.

I got on well with Sandy. Even before he changed course to become a full-time minister, it was clear that he was a devout Christian, so I was always careful not to swear in front of him. Then one day he invited me to see him perform in court. I was astonished to hear him open with: 'My Lord, this is a shithouse case.' His address continued in the same vein, peppered with a string of swear words! I relaxed with him after that.

A few years later he invited me to an Alpha Course supper to see if I would be interested. But that kind of Christianity with its absolute beliefs was not for me. Over the years my faith in any one God has diminished, but my desire to help others has not. I am now a paid-up member of the British Humanist Association, and for a few years I sponsored their Director of Music. In a nutshell, humanists believe if we all lead honest, generous lives and try to help each other, everyone will be much happier. It fits in with my logical view of life.

The Reed Foundation has a very simple mission statement, which gives total flexibility. It is that the money should be used: 'For such charitable purposes as the settler may in writing from time to time in his absolute discretion direct and after the settler's death as the trustees may in their absolute discretion decide.' In other words, I am in control – after all, it is my money. We employ no staff and all administrative work is carried out by my personal assistant. Decisions are made by the four trustees – me and my three children.

I put the money into a foundation because I believe it is important to separate the decisions about the amount you give to charity and where it should go. Once you have decided how much you want to give away, it is easier to focus on which charities should benefit. This separates the spending from the giving. I practise this with the company as well. From the mid 1970s, the policy has been to donate 1 per cent of Reed's pre-tax profits to the Charities Aid Foundation.

CHAPTER 9

Coping with crisis

I HAD REMAINED A TORY SUPPORTER from my days in the Young Conservatives, although I had not played an active part since I started Reed. What happened in the early 1980s in Britain was so painful that it shook my faith in free-market capitalism. In the short term, it also showed that giving my staff free shares was not the smartest thing to do, because they saw them fall heavily. However, those who held them for a few years eventually made good profits.

In my enthusiasm, I failed to grasp just how badly our business would be hit by the recession. Instead of retrenching, cutting back on staff and closing marginal branches, I continued to expand, opening nine new employment agency branches and eight new Medicare outlets in prime sites, bringing the total to 29. It was one of my biggest mistakes, and nearly cost me the company. Pre-tax profits plunged from £3.1 million to a mere £249,000, and we skipped the final dividend. As the major shareholder, this hit me and my family trusts more than anyone.

On the tenth anniversary of our flotation, and despite the plummeting profits, I was able to tell shareholders that our net assets had risen tenfold to £5.1 million. But prospects for 1981 were bleak and I have never believed in ambiguity. 'A group loss is forecast for the first half of the year,' I wrote in my chairman's statement, going on to thank staff for their co-operation in introducing economies including a six-month salary freeze.

Sure enough, we made a pre-tax loss of £1.64 million, the first in our history. I had made a point of telling investors that although Medicare made pre-tax losses, it made post-tax profits because of the allowances we received on opening new shops. It also gave us some tax shelter for the main business, so we paid very little tax overall. But now we were making a loss there was no war chest of paid tax to reclaim, so the recession hit us harder than competitors that had been paying a full tax charge for the preceding few years. To finance our expansion we had also built up debt of more than £2 million.

We banked with Barclays and Midland, both with regional head offices in Windsor, where Reed was also based.

I went to have a pre-Christmas lunch and discuss the situation with the manager at Midland. 'What does next year look like?' he asked. I told him it was going to be tough, but I believed we would survive. 'We have a one million pound overdraft with you and we have a million with Barclays,' I said. Then I added: 'But I may well be coming and asking for half a million more, as I will with Barclays.' He did not appear to flinch, and we finished our conversation amicably. We said 'goodbye' and wished each other 'happy Christmas' and I returned to my office believing that the job was done. How wrong I was. Within half an hour a director of Midland was on the phone asking to come and see me immediately.

He arrived thirty minutes later and told me there was no chance of Midland lending us any more money – in fact, he would probably be asking for the overdraft back. After that meeting, I rang a more senior director I knew, but he said he was no longer involved in that side of the business and could do nothing for me – so much for personal connections!

My wife will tell you that at times of great stress or excitement I have trouble sleeping. That afternoon's conversations put paid to several nights' rest. I felt more concerned about the future of the business than at any time before or since. After a worrying Christmas, in trepidation, I went to see Richard Parrish, the Barclays' director in charge of our loan. To my huge relief he was much more sympathetic and helpful. 'Don't worry about it, Alec,' he said reassuringly, 'we will lend you the entire three million.'

I realised later that Midland's stance had as much to do with its own financial problems as with ours; that taught me that banking is, like everything, an imperfect market. And so we lived to tell the tale and I went back to sleeping properly, although it was not until 1983–4 that we returned to profitability as the recession dragged on and on. I remember that time as my fraught forties and so do my family!

Our competitors, Brook Street and Alfred Marks, also suffered as corporate Britain shed staff and the market for temporaries collapsed. But Reed was particularly vulnerable with high debts and an inability to claw back tax. At one point in early 1983 our shares plunged to 19p, and one financial analyst predicted that Reed was heading for the morgue; it was certainly in intensive care.

In an industry where the costs are fixed, I had no option but to close agency branches. During 1982 and 1983 I slashed the total from 130 to 78, mainly closing those in depressed inner-city areas. I hated doing it, but the survival of the company depended upon it, as I tried to explain to our staff. The consequent reduction in costs released several million pounds of cash into the business, which kept us going.

By mid 1983, even the faith of our manager at Barclays had been stretched. When he realised that we were still struggling, he told me that his head office needed some 'comfort' that Reed was not in danger of foundering. So I commissioned a report on the company's finances by our auditors, Coopers & Lybrand. Luckily for me it took a long time to put together. When the report finally emerged, it gloomily predicted that if we did not sell some properties, or even put Medicare up for sale, we would be in real financial trouble. In other words, we might default on our loan from Barclays, which by then stood at more than £3 million. Barclays' executives were naturally dismayed and so we said that we would sell Medicare if necessary, which seemed to satisfy them.

Timing is everything – as well as luck – and those earnest experts at Coopers misread the future economy. That autumn, just after they produced the report, our business just took off. I complained to our man at Coopers, pointing out that the analysis had been badly flawed, and asked for the £25,000 fee back. Coopers refused to return any part of the fee, so we changed auditors to Robson Rhodes. We stayed with them for a long time, although now we are with Deloitte. Even in good times I do not believe in getting too close to suppliers, no matter how grand or well established they are. They should not feel too secure, otherwise complacency and sloppiness creep in.

It seemed that despite our hopes that Medicare would provide a contra-cyclical balance, Reed would always be a barometer of the overall economy. The period from the middle of 1980 to 1983 was tough for everyone except insolvency lawyers. Determined to rein in inflation, the Thatcher government put interest rates up to such an extent that even the chairman of ICI, at that time a bellwether of UK industry, complained. Many manufacturing companies ceased to exist and the industrial unrest came to a head in the miners' strike in 1984. At Reed we could not escape from the rollercoaster ride.

When, finally, demand began to recover, led by a need for temps, we found a different kind of temp was needed compared with just three years previously. Copy typists and tea ladies had all but disappeared, the first eclipsed by word processing, the second by cost cutting during the recession. Vending machines became increasingly popular. We recognised that since the introduction of desk-top computers, workers needed new skills. We started offering applicants training in word processing and data management to meet the new demands.

We changed our financial year end and reported on 15 months to March 1984 when, after two years of horrific losses, we were able to show a pre-tax profit of £1.2 million. Anyone who had bought at 19p in early 1983 was looking very clever by April 1984, when our shares had recovered to 103p. As the 1980s Thatcher boom took hold, our shares rocketed further to hit a high of 180p in early 1987.

Looking back I see that my forties were incredibly stressful and my family and colleagues had to put up with some volatile moods. Yet we kept the company afloat In a sea of troubles and once the economy turned we took it to record profits.

* * *

Somehow I still found time for charity work. Once you have experience in running charities you become a magnet for organisations in need of good management. That is how I came to join the board of Help the Aged and discovered the work of the founder, an extraordinary character and serial philanthropist called Cecil Jackson-Cole, who had also founded Oxfam in 1942.

One day in 1985 two of his executives came to see me at my office in Windsor. They wore raincoats and looked quite sinister. But instead of asking me for money, they wanted to know if I would be interested in giving my services to Jackson-Cole's charitable organisation. I went to a meeting with them and told them I was interested in the developing world, so they asked me to join the board of Helpage International, the overseas arm of Help the Aged.

It turned out that they were on the point of closing Helpage in Canada, which had been running a deficit for several years. Luck was on my side as I happened to know a talented Barbadian-Canadian businesswoman, Betty Gittens, whom I persuaded to take charge and reorganise the charity. She did a brilliant job and soon restored it to financial health.

Jackson-Cole was a fascinating man. Born in 1901 in Forest Gate, London, and named Albert Cecil Cole, he was the son of a furniture dealer. He had an unsettled childhood, as his father moved around so much that he spent less than a year at each of the many schools he attended. He left school at 13, beginning work as an office junior at the Tooley Street branch of the general provision merchants George and John Nickson, near London Bridge. Yet over the next five years he showed such talent for business that by the age of 18 he had become the owner and manager of Andrews Furnishers at Highbury Corner, Islington, which specialised in carpets.

He was devoted to his mother, whose maiden name was Jackson, and in 1927 he changed his name in her honour to Cecil Jackson-Cole when she died. The following year, aged 28, he enrolled at Balliol College, Oxford, as an external student to study economics and improve his business skills.

A few years after the end of the Second World War, he realised that in order to sell furnishings and carpets it paid to be near the people who had new premises. So he started a flat agency so that when he sold a flat he could also sell carpets to the new owners.

That business grew and became Andrews Estate Agency. He ran it and used the profits to fuel his philanthropy. He formed three charitable trusts to be the main shareholders in Andrews. These were the Phyllis Trust, named after his late first wife, which I had renamed World in Need, the Christian Book Promotion Trust and the Christian Initiative Trust.

As well as Oxfam and Help the Aged, which he started in 1961, Jackson-Cole also founded Action Aid in 1973 as well as a number of smaller charities. He put people on Andrews' payroll, but used them to work for the charities. Despite his good works he managed by divide and rule and when I went on board I found that a number of his people were at loggerheads with each other. Nevertheless, he was a remarkable character who refused all public honours for his work. Sadly, I never met him, although I did meet his widow, Theo, a few times.

In 1986 I recruited a new chief executive for Reed, with the aim of looking for a new business experience. I had in mind a short sabbatical and while I was exploring the possibilities, I became aware that Andrews itself was in financial trouble. So I asked if there was anything I could do.

Andrews had been losing money for years. The board was about to appoint as managing director a young man who had his own small chain of estate agencies. They had also sounded out an older man who knew nothing about the business to take over as chairman, as the existing chairman, Raymond Andrews, wanted to retire. I went to see Andrews and Lesley Swain, whom Jackson-Cole had put in to run Oxfam, and persuaded them that I would be good at sorting the company out.

They agreed, and I wrote my own job specification, which was: company doctor, chairman and chief executive. Hardly surprisingly, the chairman elect was annoyed, but I had my way eventually. The shareholders were the three Christian charities together with some family members. To begin with everything went well; I turned the business around and we got on with developing it.

Andrews had an expensive head office in Theobalds Road in London, miles away from any of its estate agencies. I closed that, extended the year-end by six months and put all the company losses into that period – what is known in the City as 'kitchen sinking it'.

We put in financial controls and took out the unnecessary costs to transform Andrews from making a loss of £297,000 in 1985 to making a profit of just over £1 million in 1986. The business made more than £1 million for the next three years. Once we were in profit, the company bought out the family shareholders and cancelled the shares, so that Andrews was then 100 per cent owned by the three Christian charities. Most of the non-executive directors were also devout Christians who prayed before every meeting. Despite this I found them extremely difficult to deal with in the subsequent discussions.

Soon after I arrived, we received an offer to buy Andrews. The directors were all for selling but I felt that was totally against what Jackson-Cole would have wanted. It became a real power struggle between me and them. In fact, that episode may have been the beginning of my disillusionment with Christianity.

In the end though, I got my way. I trawled through the articles of association and discovered that there were not as many members of Andrews staff on the Trust's board as there were supposed to be. By bringing in some new directors who wanted to keep the business, I managed to swing the vote in favour of rejecting the offer. The others fought me at every turn but I won the day and plucked a young man called Michael Robson from the ranks, making him managing director. He made a tremendous success of the company and was still there in 2011.

Andrews continues to support numerous charities such as Excellent Development, which helps community groups in rural Kenya, and a project that focuses on combating repeating patterns of homelessness in the UK. Andrews also supported the work of Dr Patrick Dixon, who founded ACET International, a charity that helps and provides education for Aids sufferers.

For me the most interesting thing about Andrews was discovering that there were so many similarities with running the employment agency business. The average invoice value was about the same; 25 per cent of sales fell through in both businesses; both employ and serve the same kind of young people. We helped the business to expand into South London, starting in Putney and bringing the total number of Andrews' branches to 45.

My battles at Andrews, however, added to the strain of running Reed and Medicare.

CHAPTER 10

Cancer and beyond

IN 1986 I BEGAN TO FEEL UNWELL. There was no sudden weight loss or any other specific symptom, but I gradually became aware that I simply did not feel as I should. I had a couple of medicals – in fact, I started to look for excuses to have medicals – and each time the doctors said I was fine. But I knew that, even though I was able to function in my daily life, I felt far from fine.

My GP, Geoff Baker, is a lovely man and one of my best friends. We have a jokey relationship – and nowadays I am his only patient as he retired formally some years back. He and his wife have always been close to my family; we play bridge and tennis together and I did not want to talk to him about such indeterminate feelings. Neither did I want to worry Adrianne unnecessarily.

Eventually, I had a medical at the Institute of Directors. Once again the doctor I saw after all the various tests were complete told me that all was well; this time, however, I refused to accept his conclusion. There was disquiet in my stomach area, I told him; I felt sure there was something wrong. He suggested two courses of action. The first was to see a psychologist – he pointed out that the stress I had been under at work could be affecting me and that perhaps I should talk it through with a professional. His second suggestion was to visit a GP in Harley Street, Dr Ken Kwok.

I visited the psychologist first, but I quickly realised that was a mistake. I had booked a minimum course of three sessions, but I lasted for only one. He tried to take me back to my childhood and imagine myself in the house in Rosemary Avenue, but I felt sure that the answer to my vague symptoms did not lie there, so I did not complete the sessions.

Next I went to see Dr Kwok, who was fantastic; I had faith in him from the start. My first visit to him, in June, came just before Adrianne and I were about to go to a wedding in America, so he gave me some medicine to tide me over while I was there and booked an appointment for me to have an examination after a barium meal for when I got back. The barium meal throws the internal workings into contrast so any problems can be more easily seen on the screen.

When he rang me with the results it was clear from his tone that they were not good, although he refrained from using the word cancer – to give patients such bad news over the phone is frowned on. Instead, he said that the scan had showed an obstruction of some kind and asked to see me the following Monday. I had no wish to spend the weekend worrying so I drove to London to see him that same evening. My worst fears were realised when he told me it was cancer. He said that the only sensible treatment was surgery.

In 1986 a diagnosis of colon cancer was still pretty much a death sentence. Tony Burke, our Medicare director, had died of cancer some months before. He showed considerable courage after being diagnosed, and once his strength began to fail he visited all the branches to say goodbye to the staff. I went with him on one of his visits and remember the journey well because his driving had become quite fast and aggressive – I am a nervous passenger at the best of times. The unworthy thought flashed through my mind that as he knew he was dying it no longer mattered to him whether the car crashed. When he died a few months later it was a great loss to Medicare and the whole group.

So I was well aware of the possible outcome. Friends who have had cancer tell me they felt terrified on hearing the news. I do not recall being frightened, but I was concerned. I was 52, with a growing business to run. My children were some way from being adults. James was working at Saatchi & Saatchi, Richard was taking his A-levels, and Alex was still a young teenager. It seemed cruel of fate to take me out of their lives and leave Adrianne on her own to look after them. I was, however, all too aware of people who had died leaving young children behind. I broke the news to Adrianne, who was utterly shocked as she had no idea there had been anything wrong.

My natural optimism soon took over and I had plenty to do before the operation, as I would be out of action for several weeks. I told my secretary that I did not want to be pitied nor written off. I was operated on at the Princess Margaret Hospital in Windsor within a week of the diagnosis.

It was good to have friends among the medical team. For some years we had been skiing with a group of medics from Windsor, so I knew a number of people involved in my operation. I asked Geoff to choose the surgeon, as the two candidates were both friends. He chose John Luck, one of our skiing group. The anaesthetist, John Raite, was another skier, as was one of the theatre nurses. Another nurse was married to our Human Resources director. So it was quite a jolly crew who gathered around the operating table. John Luck even invited Geoff to attend the operation.

I was well looked after, but the first day after the surgery passed in a blur. When John Luck began discussing what he had found in my colon, he said that the tumour was classed as a grade four cancer – the most severe type. Over a number of weeks I managed to wheedle out of them that I had only a 40 per cent chance of survival.

Nowadays, due to a change in medical practice, cancer patients are immediately given the bad news in all its stark reality, but for me, the details emerged gradually. The good news was that John Luck believed he had removed all the cancer. If I managed to survive for five years I would be in the clear, he told me. There is hardly any incidence of colon cancer recurring after five years.

Here my accountancy training really helped me to cope psychologically. I thought to myself that if there was a 60 per cent of my popping off over five years then there were 60 months to go. So I approached every month with the thought that I had a 1 per cent chance of dying in it. Looked at that way, dying was extremely unlikely, in fact I was more likely to die of something else. That is how I dealt with it, and 24 years later it is clear that the strategy worked well.

I am methodical and have always prepared for unexpected events, so there was no panic to put things in order. But before the operation I rewrote my will and made sure that if the worst did happen the family was not only provided for, but it would also be relatively simple for Adrianne to pick up the pieces and get on with life.

She was fantastic throughout, sensible and upbeat as ever, regarding the operation simply as a job that needed to be done.

We told the two older children that it was cancer, although we downplayed it as much as possible, but we felt that Alex was too young to be told the truth. I took her for a walk around the garden on the weekend before my operation and told her it was for haemorrhoids. She has since told me she sensed it was something a lot more serious and worried a lot about what it might be. When, later, the truth inevitably came out, she felt quite angry we had not been straight with her. The tactic of being matter of fact with the boys succeeded better because Richard tells me he barely remembers it.

One lesson the episode taught me, which I always pass on to friends, is that if you feel ill or suspect there is something wrong, don't just take the opinion of the first doctor you see. Keep on asking until you are satisfied. One of the reasons that British mortality rates for cancer lag behind those in both Europe and the United States is that diagnosis is often too late, when the disease has progressed.

It took three months to recover sufficiently to return to working full time. As soon as I was well enough to travel, we decamped to the Provence Hotel in Juan les Pins for two weeks' convalescence. While we were there we received the excellent news that Medicare had been sold for £20 million on a price/earnings ratio of 58.3 – about three times the market average at the time.

In September, three months after the surgery, Adrianne and I celebrated our silver wedding anniversary by throwing a big party on the Thames aboard the elegantly kitted out *Silver Barracuda*, a lovely boat with a striking art deco interior. All the doctors involved in the operation came to celebrate our anniversary and my recovery. Adrianne, Alex and I went to Canary Wharf to pick up the boat while it cruised up to Charing Cross Pier where we welcomed our 100 guests, all in dinner jackets and elegant dresses. On board we had the Dark Blues Orchestra playing songs from all my favourite musicals. Just as we were about to pull away from the pier there were explosions all over the sky. Ken Livingstone was throwing a farewell party for the Greater London Council, which Margaret Thatcher had disbanded. As a final gesture of defiance, he discharged an extravagant amount of Londoners' money in a huge firework display, which all aboard the *Silver Barracuda* enjoyed.

It was a great party for me. I had my wife, my children and friends around me, I felt healthy for the first time in several years, and I had got shot of Medicare for an astonishing price.

* * *

The 1980s were boom times in Britain, and once again Reed rode the wave of national prosperity. In the financial year to March 1987 our pre-tax profits more than doubled to £6.5 million and we opened more than ten new branches around the country, including Edinburgh, the City of London and even one in fashionable South Molton Street in Mayfair. The company donated 1 per cent of pre-tax profits to the Charities Aid Foundation, as it had for several years. This time it was a record £65,000.

Our share price had not yet caught up with the times, and during the year the Reed Foundation bought 10 per cent of the group's shares. That meant that nearly 70 per cent of the stock was owned by me, my children and the foundation.

Stock market analysts understood from our purchase that we felt the shares were cheap, and began to revalue them. They soared during the summer of 1987 until 19 October, otherwise known as Black Monday, when stock markets in New York and London plummeted, taking most of the markets around the world with them. The FTSE 100 plunged by more than 20 per cent in three days.

By the end of October, the London stock market had dropped by 26 per cent and Wall Street by 23 per cent. The Black Monday crash was the largest one-day fall in stock market history. Though our shares were hit along with the market, it did not affect our everyday employment business that much.

During 1986, I had made Chris Kelly managing direc-tor of Reed Recruitment. He had joined us the year before from an advertising background. He had a lot of charm and was also extremely energetic, and after my surgery I decided to make him managing director of the whole group while I kept the title chairman and chief executive. He had equal status to Derek Beal, the finance director. In an ideal world I would have preferred to bring James in at that stage, but he was still too young and inexperienced. In effect, Chris ran the operations, and as a true advertising man he enjoyed entertaining the clients. One summer he had organised a package deal from a small-time entrepreneur for a marquee at Wimbledon including lunch and tickets for Centre Court.

He invited senior managers from our top recruiters, but after lunch, while they went to watch the tennis, he stayed behind and watched horse racing, which he loved, on the television in the marquee. Imagine his embarrassment when two of his guests returned accompanied by policemen; they had been arrested for having fake tickets. The chap who had organised the package had been scammed. Chris gave him a hell of a time, but, to his credit, he came up with genuine men's final tickets for both clients.

I met Chris regularly to discuss our progress and I continued to visit the branches, as I had always done. I still visit them every Wednesday in my role as Founder at Large. Against my better judgement – I have never seen the point of non-executive directors – I made another concession to my health and to the changing climate of governance by appointing two non-executive directors. They were Tony McBurnie, then the director general of the Institute of Marketing, and Brian Ward-Lilley, a director of Barclays Bank, which had been so supportive during our own near nemesis. He, however, had not been personally involved.

During the booming 1980s Reed had accumulated a handy cash pile of £6 million, which I had kept liquid due to my distrust of equities. My caution was well placed, as we would have lost nearly £2 million in the 1987 crash had that money been invested in the market. Although dramatic at the time, the measures taken by the government to avert recession meant that the crisis lasted no more than a few weeks, and Reed sailed through it unscathed. We opened a further 22 branches that year, bringing the total to 149, although some specialist branches shared premises. The Reed name gained even greater prominence, dominating the competition, and all seemed well. Filled with optimism, I wrote in my chairman's statement for the year to March 1988: 'The opportunities open to us in our core business appear endless.'

CHAPTER 11

Student life

IN 1987 JAMES WAS 24, working for Help the Aged in Pakistan, and waiting to start an MBA course at Harvard Business School. If any of my children were going to join me at Reed it was clear that James would be the one. Richard had no business ambitions and Alex, still a teenager, looked likely to pursue a more artistic career. People say that James is most like me in character. My flirtation with death had forced me to think about the succession, but I was in no hurry to push him into the business. After Harvard he went to work for the BBC as a trainee producer and stayed for four years.

During 1988, his first year at Harvard, I joined him briefly for the entrepreneurs' course. It is called an OPM, standing for Owner/President Management Programme, and runs for three weeks for three consecutive years. After surviving cancer I decided that signing up for three years would be a good sign of my faith in the future. All the students had to submit a brief summary of their careers and achievements to date along with a picture of themselves. Everyone else sent a photo, but to be different I sent a

cartoonist's impression of my face – it certainly differentiated me from everyone else. I found the academic side of
the course stimulating, particularly the case studies. At the
end, one of the professors told us, 'Fifty per cent of what we
have studied is rubbish; it is up to you to work out which
fifty per cent.'

One surprise was the accommodation, which was surprisingly pokey and uncomfortable. Half a dozen of us
shared a communal bathroom and the beds were short,
especially for someone who is 6ft 2in tall. I was not alone
in my discomfort – a few people even decided not to return
the following year. Many of those on the course said in the
follow-up survey that they got most out of the associated
networking, but I found that the least rewarding of all.
Although I am gregarious and have many friends, I find
most Americans quite daunting socially and I struggle to
connect with them.

Harvard was my first taste of being an undergradu-
ate, but not my first experience of academia. In 1979 I had
received a letter out of the blue from the principal of Royal
Holloway, one of the largest colleges of London University,
asking me to consider becoming a member of its governing council. My brother John used to handle all Royal Holloway's printing so I assumed they had made a mistake and
that the letter was intended for him. But when I rang the
principal's secretary to check she said no, the invitation was
extended to me, and they knew exactly who I was.

I was flattered. Founded by the Victorian entrepreneur
Thomas Holloway, who made his fortune in patent medi-
cine, the college seemed to fit perfectly with my own history.
Even better, the imposing gothic building, set in wonderful

grounds, was a short walk from where we lived in Engle-field Green, so once I got over my surprise at being asked, I accepted the invitation. Quite soon afterwards the chairman of Royal Holloway's finance committee died and I took over that role.

I also helped with the details of the 1985 merger of Bedford women's college, which fitted well. Royal Holloway had originally been set up exclusively for women, but it had started admitting men in 1965. By the mid 1980s, when my business was booming again, the council had made me a Fellow, but I wanted more active involvement. I find sitting in meetings deliberating unsatisfying. Going to Harvard had whetted my appetite for teaching.

The principal of Royal Holloway in 1990 was Dorothy Wedderburn, who had been the principal of Bedford College. She introduced me to Charles Harvey, who had just been appointed head of the newly formed Royal Holloway School of Management, effectively London University's business school. Professor Wedderburn was succeeded by Norman Gower, who was given the task of setting up new departments in media studies, management studies and economics. When I suggested that Royal Holloway should introduce an entrepreneurs' course that would stimulate the students' ideas on innovation and enterprise, he encouraged me to talk to Charles.

Charles was keen to have real business people on board to give the management school credibility. As well as me he also had George Cox, who became director general of the Institute of Directors, and Phillip Crowson, then the finance director of Rio-Tinto Zinc. We made ourselves available to advise Charles over the years, and I was able to lend some financial support to the management school by buying some basic books to get the library started.

I also wanted to help raise the profile of the school so I started an annual lecture. I would invite well-known businessmen to speak at a meeting for around 250 people, which was followed by a reception. Colin Marshall, the former chairman of British Airways, gave one lecture, as did David Elstein, then at Channel 5. Several others also gave their time, including Martin Marshall, a professor from Harvard. It all helped generate publicity and raise the management school's profile.

Charles and I had several discussions about an entrepreneurs' course, and from that evolved the idea of an interactive workshop for undergraduates. He felt a course to promote management initiative was important for the future of the college. I enjoyed being part of the management school at the beginning, and I stayed actively involved for the first decade of its existence.

I knew roughly what I wanted to teach, but what to call the course? Charles left it to me. I toyed with 'Innovation and Enterprise', but that sounded insipid – like a glass of plain tonic water. It needed something stronger, a metaphorical slug of gin, to make it stand up; finally I came up with the extra ingredient – leadership. I called the course LIES – Leadership, Innovation and Enterprise Studies. And that is how someone who had failed his 11-plus and left school at 16 became a university professor!

I asked my children's advice before I started teaching. I remember Alex telling me not to expect any input from the students, but the students' participation was everything – that is how I ran it. I never wrote anything down, but I produced different exercises and topics for discussion. Every fifteen minutes the tempo changed.

One exercise would involve getting a group of three or four students to read a chapter of a book and then dramatically present a situation. We had lots of role play, and one scenario was even part of the final examination.

On one occasion the guys making the presentation all played rugby. The formed a human mountain and the smallest climbed up and balanced on top.

I wanted to introduce the students to the basics of business life, so I insisted they all turn up on time. Anyone late was fined £1, which went towards the 'toffee fund'. We did not have any facilities for a coffee break so we had 'toffee breaks'. If someone said something particularly clever or funny I would toss them an extra toffee. The sessions were really lively. I loved running them and the students seemed to love the course too.

One of the most demanding sessions was a mock board meeting. I would split the students into two groups. One group would play the directors of a real public company board, discussing the actual report and accounts of the company at a board meeting; students in the other group would observe and mark. Then they would switch places. Marks would be given out of ten, but I would only allow two nines, two eights and so on, so they really had to concentrate. It was exhausting for everyone.

I think I was able to give undergraduates a sense of what real business life was like – so many young people have no idea. For instance, I remember one session when Reed representatives were in court over litigation with American Express, so I asked a colleague to ring me from the courtroom with the verdict. As I had hoped, the call came while I was teaching and the students got the news in real time, which they found quite exciting.

LIES was an instant success and became the management school's most popular course for six years. It was always oversubscribed, as there was only room for 25 students in each of the two workshops I ran on a Friday. At the end of the day the students would be invited to a session with a guest speaker, so Fridays were exhausting but very satisfying.

In the mid 1990s I introduced a similar course to Guildhall University, which became Metropolitan College London; there it was called BABE, standing for BA in Business Enterprise. I helped set up the course, but although they also appointed me professor, I did not teach there.

One of my favourite topics was the increasing need for brain power over manpower as Western countries moved from relying on basic manufacturing to more sophisticated manufacturing and service industries. It inspired me to write my book *Capitalism is Dead; Peoplism Rules – Creating Success Out of Corporate Chaos.* In it I put forward the case that we have to create a learning culture in our businesses because skills and creativity have become so much more important to them than just mere capital. I wrote that book because I believe passionately that the future is in the hands of the gifted, irrespective of gender or race.

Everyone who joins Reed is given a battery of tests from overall IQ to psychometric assessments of different skills. It seems to me that if you have intelligent staff they will devise new approaches, new ways of doing things. Reed was the first employment agency company to recruit graduate trainees.

Most of our management team are graduates and they are given proper training in various aspects of the business. They have to go out into the branches and find out what it is like to deal with clients and candidates. Reed does not lay down strict codes of conduct and there are no manuals governing staff behaviour. Our staff need to be good at dealing with people and they also have to be intelligent. I don't believe in manuals, I believe in an intelligent response.

I naturally have one or two smaller hobby horses. One is BUDI, which stands for 'Bet You Drop It'. I would come up with an idea and because I was the boss they would say, 'Oh yes, that's great.' But as soon as my back was turned they would go back to doing what they always do.

For a few of my students, taking the LIES course changed their lives. One young man who was struggling with his maths course was sufficiently enthused by his time on LIES to become a highly successful entrepreneur. He formed an information security technology company and had a turnover in millions within a couple of years.

Teaching lively young minds was a fabulous experience. I cannot say the same about my involvement with politics, despite it beginning well.

CHAPTER 12

Flirting with politics

I HAVE ALWAYS FOLLOWED the political news, and I enjoyed my years in the Young Conservatives, although my motives for joining were as much social as anything else. In a way, once I had met Adrianne that evening in 1959, the organisation had served its purpose. After starting Reed in 1960, I became immersed in my business and then family life as well, and I gave up any commitments to the Young Conservatives.

The Labour Party had few attractions for an entrepreneur at that time. Swingeing taxation, red tape and opposition to temps, who were viewed by the trade unions as potential strike breakers, all made our life difficult. Once the Conservatives regained power in 1979, I saw how Margaret Thatcher helped to revitalise the entrepreneurial spirit, dismantling the shackles of high taxation and trade union bullying and allowing wealth creation to flourish. I disliked some of her more brutal policies, particularly towards the traditional industries, but I could see that for Reed as a business she was good news.

But once Thatcher had gone, pushed out by the 'men

in suits', I became increasingly disillusioned with the Conservative Party. It seemed to lose impetus and direction, and I found all the allegations of sleaze and scandal distasteful. Even so, I accepted a CBE under John Major's government, as it was awarded largely as a result of the efforts of Mike Whittaker and Vera Cummings, a former member of my staff and a staunch Conservative. They had both lobbied hard for me to receive an honour. (Vera later celebrated her 101st birthday in 2010.)

My connection with the Labour Party began by accident. In 1994 a very right-wing acquaintance made a generous donation to Ethiopiaid of £50,000. Soon after, I received a letter from Conservative Central Office saying he had put me forward as a potential member of the 'Thousand Club', which is made up of people who have donated £1,000 or more to the Conservative Party. I was uneasy about this, because by then there were so many sleazy stories about Conservative MPs, but he had been so generous that I felt I could hardly refuse. Despite my misgivings, I sent off a cheque for £1,000, but I felt rather unclean. As a sort of moral cleansing, I sent £1,000 to the Labour Party as well. The reactions from the two parties were dramatically different. The Conservatives sent a standard thank-you note, but Labour treated me like a new best friend, which I confess I found intriguing.

I received an invitation to the Labour Party conference that autumn, which is where I first met Sarah Macaulay (later Sarah Brown). She was one half of the public relations firm Hobsbawm Macaulay, which was working for the Labour Party, in particular handling fund raising. We got on very well – I found her intelligent and warm, and she had a good sense of humour. She would ring up with various invitations, and I started attending Labour's annual conferences with one or other of my children. Adrianne meanwhile remained faithful to the Conservatives and viewed my new relationship with Labour with some detachment – by now she had grown used to my enthusiasms. I reckoned the party conferences were educational for the children, and they seemed to enjoy them. On one occasion when I was in Blackpool with Alex we had tea with Tony Blair, which was really exciting for her, although her main recollection is that he looked orange from the make-up he was wearing, as he had just done a TV interview.

I can also reveal that one unpopular policy on taxation introduced by the Liberal Democrats in 2010 was being rattled around by Labour's policymakers as far back as 1996, before they were elected the following year. I remember attending a press conference, at Tony Blair's invitation. As the officials were handing out a briefing sheet on how they were going to tax the rich, I noticed what I thought had to be a mistake, so I called one of the officials over. 'You are talking about cracking down on tax avoidance here – surely you mean tax evasion?' The official grinned and said, 'That's no mistake. We mean tax avoidance.' This was not great news for me personally, as I have always believed that avoiding paying unnecessary tax legally – or tax planning as my accountant calls it – was simply good housekeeping. But at the time of writing, in 2011, the idea has still not made it to the statute book.

One day I was having lunch with Sarah at the Soho House club, and we fell to discussing a big Labour Party dinner that was coming up. She then told me in strictest confidence that she and Gordon Brown had started going out together, but as their relationship was still a secret she could not be seen arriving with him. I had been given two tickets for the dinner, and I knew that Adrianne would not dream of coming. So I said to Sarah, 'Why don't you come with me?'

She agreed, and so for that one night I was a cover for Gordon Brown. Sarah arrived with me and went home with him – and I have to confess that I enjoyed playing my part in this clandestine affair.

Through Sarah I had several meetings with Gordon Brown, whom I liked. In private he was intellectually stimulating, without pretence and surprisingly good fun – very unlike his public image. When tragedy struck after they married and they lost their first baby, I wrote a letter of sympathy and mentioned that my son Richard and his wife Lisa had just gone through a similar experience. Their son, Adam, died after just two weeks struggling for life. Despite their own grief, Gordon and Sarah wrote a warm letter to Richard and Lisa, which I know they have kept.

Sometimes I was invited to speak at Labour business meetings on enterprise. As I normally do, I would tell the story of how I built Reed up from one office into the best-known employment agency in Britain. I have always enjoyed talking to an audience, and I found those meetings especially stimulating.

There is no doubt that Sarah opened doors to places where I could not have gone without her: dinners and lunches with top politicians and business leaders. I became quite an enthusiast, and as a result of what I heard at these occasions, I decided to donate £100,000 to the party, on top of other, smaller donations I had made along the way. But little did I realise that by becoming a Labour Party donor I was putting myself right in the firing line of Labour's enemies in the press, most notably *The Mail on Sunday*.

CHAPTER 13

A family business

MY BRUSH WITH CANCER made me think increasingly about succession in the business. I would be 60 in February 1994, and James would be 31 in a couple of months, so if he was going to lead the company time was pressing. Through the early 1990s he was working happily at the BBC, even though the pay was low and he found the politics of the organisation tricky. James said when he left university that he wanted to stay independent until he was 30, but, although that birthday had passed, he was still undecided. In 1992, I asked him to become a non-executive director of Reed to give him some inside knowledge of how the company worked. He went along with it, but I could see no evidence of real enthusiasm.

Then fate played into my hands. The BBC put a lot of its programme makers out to contract, including James. He was not impressed, particularly when he was turned down for a job on The Money Programme.

He and a friend made a programme for the BBC called 'Crazy Ways for Crazy Days' about Tom Peters, the American business guru. The programme was a great success, making around £1 million for BBC Enterprises, but when James and his friend asked the BBC for money to make a similar programme they were turned down. James felt, as have so many before and since, that the BBC was a creative business being run like the civil service.

Meanwhile, we had a senior vacancy for an operations director that I thought would suit him. We talked about it, but he would not give me a definite decision so, slightly frustrated, I placed an advertisement in the *Sunday Times* for the position. That Sunday morning I handed him the newspaper and said: 'You had better look for your job in the appointments section.'

It did the trick. Once he saw I was prepared to hand the job to an outsider he realised he did want to become part of the company. I felt it was a gamble worth taking. If James was up to the job, he would stay; if he failed in some way or just did not fit in, he could leave.

He joined full time in April 1994 – the day before his 31st birthday – as operations director of Reed Employment. He witnessed the ups and downs of Reed at a particularly volatile time, which was excellent experience for him. His timing was spot on as we were about to enter the most profitable period of our history so far.

By 1995 James had proved himself a capable manager and moved up to being chief operating officer. It would be disingenuous to pretend that Chris Kelly was not unsettled by the progress James made and, in fairness, he was in a difficult position. I believed that there was room for them both, but understandably Chris felt threatened. In the end, they began to get in each other's way.

In late 1997 I bit the bullet and asked Chris Kelly to

resign and James stepped into his shoes as chief executive.

To mark the event I gave James a conductor's baton. I said at the time that he had the precision of a musician whereas I have more of a painter's broad brush approach. Where I am instinctive, he is cerebral and strategic. He had the baton framed and keeps it high on his office wall to remind him of his responsibilities.

Of course it was nepotism. My brother John disapproved – neither of his children took over the reins at his company – and we received mixed press reviews about the move. We were, after all, still a public company even if the family held the majority of the shares.

Emotionally I wanted my son to head the group and once he was in the job, I felt Reed's future as a family business was assured.

I always wanted the company to have the values of a family business – focused on the long term rather than making a quick buck. An outsider as chief executive faces more pressure to succeed in the short term, perhaps to the detriment of the ultimate value of the company. Having a member of the Reed family at the top also cuts out a lot of company politics; executives know that James will not be headhunted, so jockeying for position is no longer relevant.

James and I worked well together. In the beginning, I would ask his opinion on various issues but then I would make the decisions; by the time I stepped down from the chairmanship in 2003 the roles were reversed – he would ask my opinion but he would make the decisions. I am not sure at what point the switchover occurred, but it is certainly the case now.

All the directors realised it was a risk and we were both anxious about how we would get on. Business manuals are full of warnings about fathers and sons running businesses together. On the other hand Sainsbury's, Wal-Mart and Marks & Spencer are examples of how family businesses prospered through the generations.

James told me later that he felt I would be a very difficult act to follow. He did not want to mess up, and most of all he did not want to ruin our relationship.

It was naturally challenging for me to stand back and relinquish control. But I had already done that to an extent with Chris Kelly and Romney Rawes before him. James is more of a strategic thinker than me. Even now, I continue to come up with new ideas and some James will embrace and make happen, while others he will quietly forget.

Bringing a child into a business has many advantages as well as potential pitfalls. James had grown up around the business. He had visited branches, worked in Medicare in the holidays and had been instilled with the Reed culture when he was a boy.

At Reed I have always insisted that the staff look smart. Chris Kelly took it a step further by making a rule that the men should wear a dark suit and a company tie with the ubiquitous three red dots, and the women formal clothes and preferably a company scarf, although this is rarely adhered to. Punctuality is a given, along with 'intelligent response'. James had absorbed the company culture. One of my mantras is 'What the hell is going on?' None of this did I have to explain to James.

We also had the luxury of spending time together outside business hours. We both love horses and, as I have mentioned, many important business decisions were made on our weekend morning rides in the Cotswolds.

Best of all, delegating day-to-day responsibility meant I was able to spend more time developing ideas for my Foundation.

CHAPTER 14

Ethiopiaid

OUTSIDERS MIGHT ASSUME that I put my £5 million from the sale of Medicare into the Reed Foundation out of gratitude for coming through cancer. Perhaps subconsciously that played a part, but I was not aware of it. For me it was more to do with not wanting to give the taxman 40 per cent of the money in capital gains tax, not to mention a further 40 per cent in inheritance tax if I did not survive. And I had a strong desire to help to alleviate some of the horrific problems in the developing world.

Quite often after serious illness people give money to research into finding a cure for that particular malady, but my view is that cancer charities are hugely well endowed.

In my charitable giving I aim to apply the same innovative and creative skills as I do in business. And, as in business, I discovered that working in philanthropy is far from easy. In charity work, however, the problems are different to those in business. If you own the majority of the shares in a business, you make the decisions and everybody goes off and implements them – you only have to worry about your competitors. In running a charity, however, you have to take people with you because you don't have the power of ownership.

In philanthropy, I have found that the obstacles come from people who do not want to do things my way even though I am supplying the start-up money. It is all too easy to become emotionally involved in a cause, but then discover that when getting projects off the ground you come up against all kinds of practical problems. Sometimes there is a cultural clash. For instance, we in the West are very specific, but in Africa and other developing regions, people sometimes appear to us to be much more vague about what they mean, even though they seem to be speaking the same language. Nowhere did this come home to me more clearly than in Ethiopia. While I was mulling about where to put my money fate took a hand and blew a charismatic Ethiopian woman into my life who sowed the seeds of what became Ethiopiaid.

Jember Teferra came from Ethiopia's aristocracy. She had been educated in Britain and seemed to be genuinely bi-cultural. When she told me about the plight of the poor in her country I immediately wanted to help.

As a result of my activities, my children had all become interested in charity when they were growing up. James worked for Help the Aged in Bangladesh, Pakistan and Afghanaid before he went to Harvard. On one adventure he took some money into Afghanistan on a clandestine mission, dressed as an Afghan. I am glad I did not know about it at the time.

He had long been telling me that if I wanted to help in developing countries, whether it was with Helpage or Womankind, then I should visit some of them. So in the autumn of 1987 Adrianne and I accepted Jember's invitation to visit Addis Ababa, Ethiopia's capital, on what I regarded as a one-off fact-finding mission. I thought of it as a one-off trip to explore how to introduce some entrepreneurialism into communities. But it was impossible not to be moved by the appalling poverty. In one village the streets were streaming with urine and faeces from overflowing latrines and the only way to get rid of the sewage was by using a specially adapted truck to suck it up. I was so appalled we quickly bought that village a suction truck. I also gave £7,000 to re-open a garment factory that had been closed arbitrarily.

Jember was related to Haile Selassie, the former Emperor of Ethiopia, who was deposed in 1974. Her husband had been mayor of Addis Ababa and came from another grand family. One Sunday they took us into the countryside for a picnic. We drove for many miles and they told us that before the revolution all the land that we saw had been their territory. It had all been confiscated by the Communists and they had both been thrown into prison for several years.

In 1987 Jember's mission was to improve life for people living in the 'kebeles' (poor urban neighbourhoods) of Addis Ababa. In Ethiopia her friends regarded her as the 'one who goes where angels fear to tread'. She had worked as a nurse and for the Red Cross, where she had brought about many changes.

Jember is immensely impressive in her passion to alleviate the terrible conditions in her country, making her a brilliant fundraiser. People find her arguments compelling and she had persuaded the British Overseas Development Agency to match any funds she raised from non-governmental organisations (NGOs). In 1987 she submitted a

£1 million proposal for a project to redevelop three kebeles over two years in line with a previous scheme. The ODA said it might be prepared to give as much as £500,000 over five years if Jember could raise matching funds from private donors in the UK, the largest commitment it had ever made at that time.

But progress raising money from donors was sluggish – too slow for my liking. I wanted to be an active investor and I agreed to co-ordinate the donations and to underwrite the entire £500,000 to get the two-year project off the ground while we sought more donations – I knew it was just a matter of time before the money came in. By the end of 1989 we had funding commitments from Water Aid, Help the Aged and Band Aid among others, all of which agreed to visit Addis regularly to audit the project.

Jember and I then fell out dramatically over the scale of the project. We had arranged a meeting on 1 January 1990 with the entire management team and all the staff. After an hour or so of discussing various operational problems, Jember announced that the scheme was really a £5 million project over five years, not a £1 million project over two years. My recollection is that this was a complete surprise, not to say shock, to me. The project management company was charging an 18 per cent fee and had not yet built a single house, but suddenly Jember was proposing a much bigger scheme.

I was not at all confident that her team had either the experience or the expertise to complete a much bigger scheme. Everything got very emotional. I almost felt I was being accused of racism and of doubting their ability to execute a much bigger project.

I was convinced we should complete the original project first and then think about what else we could do. I knew that the ODA would want to see one project completed before it would give us any more money and I knew it had strict accounting and reporting standards.

I also discovered that Jember had been raising money from other sources without consulting me; as I was supposedly the co-ordinator I found this disconcerting. I could see the whole kebeles project spiralling out of control. In the end we agreed to disagree, other donors appeared and Jember and I went our separate ways. It was an instructive example of how plans can unravel when those who think they understand each other discover that they do not. In fact, it was so revealing that James wrote a case study on the whole project for Harvard Business School, which is still available for purchase. It was a bruising but instructive episode.

Despite this setback, I was hooked on helping to improve the lives of the poor in Ethiopia. I founded Ethiopiaid in the autumn of 1989, and over the next twenty years it donated more than £20 million to partner projects in that country. At the end of 2010, we were involved with sixteen partner projects aiming to donate about £2 million a year to these deserving causes.

I am a man of great enthusiasms, and Ethiopiaid has certainly been one of them. When I first visited the country and was taken on a tour by Jember and her husband, I was struck not just by the poverty but also by the incredible beauty of the scenery. It is a highland, mainly rural place, full of contrasts. There are awe-inspiring waterfalls and volcanic hot springs; the country contains some of Africa's highest mountains as well as some of the world's lowest points below sea level.

The indigenous population has a unique culture that differentiates Ethiopians from the rest of Africa. The Ethiopians are Semitic in origin – early pictures show the original ten tribes that came from Syria. In the earliest, the people look Mediterranean but as they integrated they became darker-skinned. The country is fascinating because it was so isolated for so long. It has its own alphabet and its own calendar. Each year has thirteen months with one of just six days – thirteen months of sunshine, they like to say. Ethiopia also has its own clock. Instead of starting and ending at midnight, the day starts at sunrise. Orthodox Christianity is the traditional religion but at least a third of the population is now Muslim. The Ethiopian version of Christianity has food laws that are akin to kosher food laws in Judaism because the early Christians were Jewish by birth.

The place is beguiling and quite different from anywhere else. I visit every other year to keep in touch with our various partners and see how the projects are doing. Adrianne sometimes comes with me, while James, his wife Nicola, and Alex have all been at their own expense. Richard likes to help by giving donations.

In 2009 James and his family visited the House of Angels, a hospice founded by Mother Teresa of Calcutta, which follows her way of working. We have supported it for some years, but that time two of my older grandchildren visited and found it very shocking. People were dying of various conditions – just packed in next to each other. Others were dying of treatable illnesses that do not really exist any more in the West. There were some 1,800 to 2,000 people being cared for by the nuns. Mother Teresa did not believe in active fund-raising, although the House of Angels does accept donations. But it will not allow its real name to be used on any leaflets nor does it have any promotional material. The guiding philosophy is 'God will provide.'

A couple of years before that I had visited the hospice, and as I was leaving I asked if there was anything they needed in particular. The head sister said that they were in desperate need of baby milk for some infants whose mothers had died. I said regretfully that I didn't know anyone in that market and she simply said: 'God will provide.'

My next appointment was a party at the British Embassy in Addis. The contrast could not have been a starker. Set in lovely lawns amid flowering borders, the residence is a solid single-storey house, built more or less symmetrically around two internal courtyards. At the top of two flights of wide steps, in season its pillared portico is covered with wistaria and the two flanking wings are ablaze with bougainvillaea for some of the year. To the right, adjoining the family rooms, a veranda giving on to the side garden runs the depth of the house. In the extensive grounds are tennis courts, a golf course and swimming pool. The former emperor, Haile Selassie, gave the land to the British for their help in fighting off the Italians.

Anyway, I was wandering about looking for someone to talk to when I spotted a couple of Brits and introduced myself. Their main business was importing Japanese 4x4 cars into Ethiopia, but almost the first thing one of them said was, 'You don't happen to know anyone who wants to buy some baby milk, do you?'

I looked heavenwards to the God I had stopped believing

in, but had to stop myself getting too excited. The chap started talking about how much he wanted for the consignment, so I said: 'Why don't you come and see the House of the Angels?' I thought that would help to beat the price down. So I took him along and he went on the tour of dying people and could not help but be moved. In the end he sold the consignment to Ethiopiaid for half price and we passed it on to the nuns. The milk had come from Japan, but although it was perfectly good most people in Ethiopia mistrusted it because it had Japanese writing on the packaging.

I like to support projects run by people I trust, such as the Addis Ababa fistula hospital. Women who have difficult births in Ethiopia sometimes develop this horrible condition – a damaged bladder which renders the woman incontinent and therefore makes her an outcast. Husbands cannot tolerate a woman with untreated fistula, so these women usually end up leading isolated lives, scratching a living and sometimes committing suicide. There are an estimated 40,000 women with fistula in Ethiopia. In the past twenty years, Ethiopiaid has donated £3 million to the Addis Ababa fistula hospital, which provides surgery to correct the condition, allowing the women to return home cured, able to start a new life.

Another horrible disease is Noma, or gangrenous stomatitis, which attacks people with immune systems weakened through malnutrition. It eats away at the flesh of the victim's face and mouth and eventually kills them. Victims are ostracised by society and lead lives of unbelievable pain and misery. Ethiopiaid has a programme of funding reconstructive operations which cost £800 each.

Reed has been involved in Ethiopia for twenty years,

during which time the population has doubled and the currency has halved in value, making improving the quality of life there an increasingly daunting task. The problem is that most people are part of an effectively medieval pastoral society trying to survive in the 21st century. Most Ethiopians are not naturally entrepreneurial, but there has been considerable outside investment, particularly from China, which has bought vast mineral deposits and built roads and other infrastructure in order to move the goods around.

Saudi Arabia is another keen inward investor, taking land on long leases from the Ethiopian government to grow food to export to Saudi. Agriculture is extremely expensive in Saudi Arabia, so the government needs alternative sources of crops. I only hope that the overall impact will be beneficial to the Ethiopian people.

CHAPTER 15

Womankind

I WAS PONDERING WHAT TO DO with the Reed Foundation's new-found wealth when I attended a Helpage International brainstorming weekend. I remember sitting in the sun daydreaming when suddenly the thought came to me that if there was an international charity especially for old people, there should also be one for women in developing countries who need help.

Reed's early success had been built on women, who made up most of our workforce and were promoted to a senior level; so I am a fan of women in general although I would not call myself a feminist. I have too many old-fashioned habits like opening doors for women and walking on the outside of the pavement for that.

Women give a lot to charities and they do put in much of the voluntary work. I felt that if you were dishing out money, it was not a bad idea to give some to women to spend, especially in Africa, which is renowned for corruption. My idea was to support a new charity for women for three years until it was well established, so I gave £1 million to set it up and to be spent on fund raising. The aim was to support women in developing countries who were suffering from abuse and neglect and from particular medical conditions that only affect women. I recruited a real tough cookie, Dr Kate Young, to be the first executive director when the charity was launched on International Women's Day in 1989.

We had quite an argument over the title. I wanted to call it Women in Need, but she felt that would make women sound helpless. She came up with Womankind, but we had to call it Womankind Worldwide to avoid clashing with the existing Womankind, which has a much narrower remit.

I thought they should use my £1 million to establish a fund-raising base by 'cold mailing' strangers, although lists from other charities could be used. The donations would go to pay for the mailing, but by getting them you identify people as serious donors. If you can then sign them up via a banker's order, the donations keep coming and typically last for six or seven years.

Kate and her team felt this approach was too risky, so in the end I let them follow their more targeted approach. They have been very effective in their later mailings and in fact I have learned a thing or two from them. Maggie Baxter, ex-Comic Relief, succeeded Kate and then Sue Turrell took over as chief executive in 2006. She had worked in international development for most of her career, spending time in the Middle East and Africa, so she had vast knowledge and experience. Her mission is to help women be less passive and Womankind supports women's organisations in places where women are oppressed.

The Womankind philosophy is that women need to be encouraged to be part of the solution. Indeed, they have withdrawn from some countries such as India and Albania because the women's movement in those countries is so vibrant and the £2.5 million they have each year will be better spent in places such as Kenya or Uganda where much still needs to be done.

Womankind works hard to roll back some cultural practices, notably female circumcision; in some societies a girl is unmarriageable if the operation has not been performed. Working with young women and helping them to say no – in some cases they form clubs known as 'Uncut clubs' – Womankind has helped reduce the rate of female circumcision from 97 per cent in one area to about 5 per cent.

A few years ago Sue and I worked on the successful merging of Womankind with Women at Risk, a charity I had started a few years previously to help women in the UK. I felt that as well as aiding women in the developing world, we should also help those in Britain who suffer abuse, mostly physical but often mental as well. Womankind has attracted a lot of bright women to the board, and patrons include the broadcaster Kate Adie, the author and broadcaster Sandi Toksvig and Lady Helena Kennedy QC.

* * *

Mistakes in charity work are inevitable, just as they are in business. I have had lots of ideas, but I have had to accept that they would not all work out.

Not long after my falling out with Jember, I read that War on Want was on the verge of bankruptcy, so I asked if I could help. A group of their people were in my office within hours and I said that I would help them – but on my terms.

War on Want had been run by ideological left-wingers.

More than a decade before he became Prime Minister, Harold Wilson came up with the name War on Want in a 1950s pamphlet for the Association for World Peace on the subject of world famine. War on Want was founded in 1954 and focused on ways of making various poor and hungry groups more self-sufficient, rather than providing emergency food aid. In the 1970s it became a co-operative, so everyone from the switchboard operator upwards was paid the same. Then in 1983 George Galloway, the smooth-talking left-winger, became General Secretary to pursue, among other things, his 'internationalism', which involved supporting regimes in Cuba, Palestine and Pakistan. However, he eschewed the frugal Maoist ways of the staff, preferring to dine in Soho restaurants and travel overseas on behalf of the charity. Shortly after he left in 1988 it became clear the charity was struggling financially and various trustees left. The remaining staff and trustees decided it could not pay its debts and had decided to wind it up.

My proposal was straightforward. I would put up £500,000 to pay off the most pressing debts to overseas projects on condition that the employees waive their rights to redundancy pay and that the existing trustees retired. I would appoint new trustees and run the charity on much better commercial terms. The problem was that War on Want was controlled by its members, whose approval was needed to get these proposals through. Some dubbed me a 'Thatcherite businessman' right from the off, and therefore regarded me as suspect. As I pointed out, I had often supported the Labour Party and had voted for Wilson, but as far as they were concerned I was a multi-millionaire capitalist and therefore the enemy.

Meanwhile, I took management control, cut the expenses and costs as I would in any loss-making business; very quickly War on Want became solvent again as the regular donations by banker's order continued to flow in. By the time an extraordinary general meeting was organised at the Conway Hall in Bloomsbury to approve our proposals, a faction inside War on Want had decided to thwart the plan.

I was more or less oblivious to this and had Hill Samuel prepare a formal document outlining the proposals. I had advertisements prepared to go into the papers the following Monday with the headline 'War on Want is Back at the Front'.

The document was sent to all members and we had postal proxy votes of 550 in favour and 75 against, so I thought we were home and dry. But the motion still had to be put to the meeting. The group opposing us, headed by a young man called Martin Hughes, told the meeting that War on Want was now solvent. Another said that the starving people of the Third World did not want money from the likes of Alec Reed. In the end, the meeting was adjourned and the motion was never put to vote. There was nothing I could do except ruefully arrange for the advertising space to be filled by ads for Ethiopiaid.

That was in 1990 and since then I have largely avoided personal controversy with my charity work. I find it easier to channel Reed Foundation money to charities I admire or those I have set up and whose management operates on an arm's-length basis.

CHAPTER 16

The roaring Nineties

THE 1990S WAS A VERY ACTIVE DECADE for the company, but it started badly. Reed's ride on the late 1980s wave of prosperity ended abruptly as we crashed into losses in 1991. But this time I had been cautious, so we were in much better financial shape than in the recession of the early 1980s. That experience instilled in me that I never wanted to be in the banks' power again. We had no debt on the balance sheet, nor did we have the loss-making Medicare. Even so, the turn-round from profit to loss was dramatic. In 1991 we changed the year end to 31 December and reported on just 39 weeks, in which we made a loss of £4.3 million before tax, which was bad enough. Unemployment in Britain rose above 2.5 million as the recession bit and the number of people employed in manufacturing in Britain fell below 5 million for the first time. The mood felt grim as the IRA renewed its attacks in London and the first Gulf War dominated the headlines.

We took quick evasive action, slashing costs, laying off staff and freezing all salaries, with the executive directors all taking pay cuts – mine was slashed by 42 per cent, the most drastic – and no dividend paid. You have to lead by example.

In the following full year, the losses increased to £5.7 million, bringing total losses for that recession to £10 million, and unemployment continued to rise. The IRA bomb in a Manchester shopping centre damaged one of our branches while another in Oxford Street was too close for comfort. The Conservatives narrowly won a fourth term of office and by the end of the year Reed's business slowly began to turn round. I said in my 1992 chairman's statement that we looked forward to contributing to the rebuilding of British industry – it had been that bad. I also said that the employment agency industry had changed more in the last three years than in the previous thirty.

Reed had been nimble in embracing those changes that were mainly about the way that big companies and state organisations operated – they now wanted exclusive contracts with employment agencies to supply temporary staff. Some of our biggest contracts today are with state employers such as the police, big chunks of the National Health Service and local education authorities. In some big companies such as Hewlett Packard we worked so closely with the HR department that we even had a de facto Reed branch inside the organisation. Chris Kelly's abundant charm made him good at marketing and negotiating these contracts, which gave our business a much more stable foundation.

The following year – 1993 (although we again changed the year end, this time to January 1994) – we were back in profit, but we still made less than £1 million.

In 1995 pre-tax profits had soared to £8.8 million on turnover of £150 million, up by 30 per cent on the previous year. James and I now faced the challenge of working closely together. We jumped in at the deep end, initiating a new wave of action. We started new ventures such as Reed Learning, Reed Graduate and Reed Managed Services.

In my efforts to be a benign employer, we had set a minimum wage within the company that applied to both permanent and temporary staff. It was only £3.10 an hour, but it was a start and was beneficial in low-paid contract work. In 1995 we also won a High Court victory against HM Customs & Excise that changed the basis of charging VAT in certain sectors. We were cleared to be able to charge VAT on only our margin instead of the full invoice value. In practice, that meant a cut of up to 15 per cent in the costs of temporary staff to some employers. Our clients were delighted.

We increased our work in prisons to help offenders become employable on release. Reed Restart provided offenders with rehabilitation and training, giving them real work to do. It may not have been the most stimulating work – stuffing envelopes with letters and a small gift such as a pen for a charity was one of the tasks – but we set targets and gave prisoners some sense of achievement. Although I accept that some criminals are so damaged and set in their ways that they will never be reformed, I believe that many people in prison could lead normal lives outside if given the right opportunity and support.

We began Reed Re-start, a not-for-profit enterprise, in Holloway Prison, but later extended the scheme to provincial gaols. At Eastwood Park women's prison near Bristol some of the inmates were a little too enterprising. We had them stuffing charity envelopes and putting them into big, strong mailbags – big and strong enough to hold a person.

One day, just after the van had picked up the mailbags, a sharp-eyed warder noticed that one of the prisoners was missing. He questioned the other girls who eventually told him that she had been smuggled out in one of the mailbags and that she was now well on her way to the sorting office. Just how she was planning to escape when the van doors were opened I have no idea, but her freedom was short lived. The van was directed back to the prison before it reached the depot.

One of our most satisfying ventures, which came a bit later, has been partnering the government in Welfare-to-Work programmes, helping to get young people back into employment. Reed was the first company in Britain to become involved.

Shortly after Labour took power in 1997, Geoffrey Robinson, the Paymaster General, asked me to meet him. He told me the Government was thinking of outsourcing some of the work of Job Centres. Would I be interested? 'Yes, very interested,' I replied promptly. Geoffrey's main proposal was to outsource work to help unemployed people get back into work. I said: 'We would love to take over one of the areas such as Surrey or Middlesex. We could make a good job of that.'

He had a less attractive proposition in mind. 'Oh no,' he said. 'We are thinking of parcelling out the most difficult cases, people who have been out of work for a couple of years or more.'

I was less enthusiastic about that idea until he mentioned that Manpower, one of our biggest rivals, was interested. I could not afford to let one of our main competitors steal a march on us and Robinson knew it.

I must have forgotten to mention this conversation

to James because the first he knew about the scheme was when he got a call in his Baker Street office from someone saying that the Paymaster General wanted to speak to him. Thinking it might be a hoax, he said he would call back. 'I looked up the Paymaster General's office on the website and rang the number,' James told me. To his surprise, he was soon talking to Geoffrey about the idea, which Labour had named the New Deal, and they agreed to meet. James did some research and realised that the plan fitted perfectly with the Reed philosophy. At the start there were just two contracts up for grabs – Humberside and Hackney; James decided to bid for the Hackney contract.

James rang Chris Melvin, the area manager of Reed Accountancy in the South East. He was keen to be involved, so they put together a small team to bid for the Hackney contract and won it. Reed in Partnership, the company formed to run it, has now grown into a substantial business and has placed more than 110,000 people, who had been long-term unemployed, in jobs. We have worked in extremely rough areas such as the Gorbals in Glasgow and inner-city Liverpool and it is really satisfying to see people regaining their self-esteem. Originally the scheme was aimed at the young, but over time it was extended to include all the long-term unemployed.

There is much more to the scheme than finding people jobs, because many of the candidates regarded themselves as 'unemployable'. When people have been out of work for a long time they become so demoralised that their confidence needs rebuilding before they can even be sent to an interview, so boosting their morale and changing their attitude is an important part of the work. Chris created a 'campus'-style office for the first Reed in Partnership operation in Hackney, designed to be relaxed, friendly and inviting. It had an internet cafe, there were banners outside and the staff all dressed in bright casual clothes. We wanted it to be as different from the depressing Job Centre experience as possible. We no longer call it a 'campus' and the offices are more conventional, but still we make sure they are welcoming.

We train the candidates quite rigorously, teaching them how to create an impressive CV and giving them plenty of interview practice so they know how to behave and react during one. We hold group sessions where candidates can role-play and compare notes, because meeting and talking to other people in the same predicament is itself a confidence booster. We also take them through the minefield of the benefit system so that they will not lose out if they start work; many people think they are better off on benefits than in a low-paid job, but we can often show them that they are wrong. The Department of Work and Pensions has produced some fascinating research showing how people benefit psychologically from working.

The Labour government paid us a fee when we placed a long-term unemployed person in a job; a further fee was paid if that person was still in the job after three months. Reed in Partnership has grown fast, and, along with our internet company, is one our most important new ventures over the past decade.

By early 2011 there were about 900 staff working in Reed in Partnership, and the company had expanded into Poland and Australia. The coalition government elected in May 2010 threw everything up in the air, as new governments tend to.

All the various job schemes under Labour were grouped into a single Work Programme and new contracts were put out to tender. Sadly the new regime refused to look at past performance as a criterion of winning the contracts and, in the main, based their decisions on cost.

Reed in Partnership lost previously held contracts, although it won the contract for the whole of West London which by coincidence covers Hounslow, where I was born and brought up.

CHAPTER 17

reed.co.uk

IN 1995 REED TOOK A FIRST, tentative step into cyber-space. That was the same year that Jeff Bezos launched Amazon in America; by 2010 Amazon had captured 50 per cent of the bookselling market. The arrival of Google was still five years away and not even Bill Gates of Microsoft or Steve Jobs of Apple had yet realised just how all-pervading the internet would become.

Even so, the dotcom fever that would dominate the next five years had begun to take hold, with new companies starting up every week. Chaos threatened, but in 1994 Tim Berners-Lee, the inventor of the World Wide Web, was persuaded to form the World Wide Web Consortium, which promoted common standards for the internet.

My view is that if a bus looks as if it is going somewhere interesting, it pays to get on it – even though you can sometimes end up walking home. To optimists such as James and me, the internet held out apparently limitless opportunities to reach our customers, but at the same time it also posed a threat to our traditional business. Job seekers accustomed to walking into a Reed agency would soon be able to look for work online, so we had to find a way of ensuring that the site they looked at was ours. Suddenly anyone anywhere could compete with us; the straitjacket of geography was broken.

Back in 1962 the Canadian educator and media guru Marshall McLuhan had said, 'The new electronic inter-dependence re-creates the world in the image of a global village.' It took more than thirty years, but his prophecy was about to be realised. We needed to catch the village bus and so reed.co.uk was formed.

Our earliest website was put together by a young IT con-tractor known as Pancake the Clown. He used to moonlight as a children's entertainer and eventually went on to make it his career. There have been ten versions of the reed.co.uk website so far, and an eleventh is under development.

The first featured so small in my mind that I did not even mention it in my 1995 chairman's statement; but I had a feeling that it was worth investing in – I felt that it was dangerous not to, because competition of any kind should never be ignored.

I love technology. Visitors to my office often express sur-prise to find me tapping away on an iPhone G4 and working on my iPad. Not many business-people in their seventies enjoy new technology in the way that I do, although there is a growing band of us. There are plenty of bright young people at the Reed Foundation who set up the new gadgets for me, which is a founder's luxury. I bought an iPad the moment it was launched in 2010 and enjoy all the apps. I have downloaded the Scrabble and Bridge apps and I am amazed by Shazam, which tells you which song or piece of music is playing, no matter where you may hear it.

If there are a few minutes spare between meetings, I practise bridge to help me win at my regular game. A group of us, including Bernard Marks, play twice a month on Thursday mornings at the RAC Club in Pall Mall, with the losers paying for lunch. But there are one or two refinements to the usual rules: for instance, if a pair makes a slam which they did not bid, they have to buy a bottle of champagne. These side bets make the game a bit more interesting – and as you may have gathered by now, I love to win.

That aside, I am quite traditional in many ways. I always wear a suit and tie in the office, and expect others to do the same. Until I received my knighthood, all the staff at Reed called me 'Mr Reed', which was a legacy from the early days when I used the title to cover my youth. I did not like it, but it helped people to differentiate between me and James, who was, and is, the boss.

I have an intensely curious mind, so I like to know about the latest 'new new' thing. Technology can create huge advantages – and I always want Reed to be in the forefront.

I do not just want to leave it to the co-members – a term we prefer to 'staff'. I want to be flexible and never to become ossified, unable to communicate with other people no matter whether they are Jon Brooks, who ran the Big Give charity, or one of my eleven grandchildren.

A technologically savvy young man called Paul Rapacioli was the first head of our internet company, reed.co.uk. Martin Warnes, who now leads it, worked with Paul at the beginning. Martin recalls that the first website showed 'lots of youthful enthusiasm' – in other words, it was light years away from the sophistication of our 2010 site. The main page featured the gold name plate that we used on all our branch doors surrounded by the various Reed logos. The visitor could find out some information about Reed and its various divisions, but that was about it. In effect, it was not much more than an electronic brochure.

The second version of the site in 1997 was a little more sophisticated. Job seekers could register and search for work and Kay, the receptionist, would type jobs on to it in between answering the phone and greeting visitors. Again there was information about the bricks and mortar business and a button named 'Intelligent Response', which summed up Reed's philosophy. At that point though, all the jobs advertised online were dealt with by our branches.

Crucially, however, the first person placed by reed.co.uk lived in Bournemouth, but the site helped him find a job in Basingstoke. That would not have happened had he walked into the local branch, so it opened my eyes to the internet's potential. Now we are truly global.

The main problem for Paul and his team back then was finding enough jobs to put on the website. Online recruitment was gaining momentum, but was still far from being the first place most job seekers would look, if indeed they had access to a computer. The team tried copying local and national press ads on to our website, but that took a lot of time to do and the information in a press ad is rather succinct because of space and cost considerations. Internet applicants want more detail.

Another experiment was to try out a website exclusively for temps. A chap from one of our competitors left his company saying the way forward for temps was on the internet and that within six months he could have such a website up and running.

My team heard about it and said they could do it in two. We let them have a shot at it and called it Tempsjobs.com. They actually beat their own estimate; I went on holiday and when I got back it was all set to go. I went to the early-morning press launch in March 2000, but only a few journalists turned up and the team gave a lacklustre presentation.

I held a post-mortem on how they could have done better, but by mid morning our share price had raced up, adding millions to the share price, such was the internet fever at the time. The excitement soon petered out, though. We spent £1.5 million on Tempjobs.com before it became clear that it was not going to make money and we closed the site.

Before this, Paul, a true lateral thinker, approached us with what sounded like a crazy idea. He suggested allowing any company, friend and foe alike, to advertise on reed.co.uk absolutely free. His belief was that a crowd attracts a crowd.

We wanted to be to recruitment what Amazon was to books – the first place job seekers and recruiters look. That became self-fulfilling once people had put our site on their 'favourites' list – whenever they needed to look at the jobs market they would start with us.

We called the service Freecruitment. Originally Paul thought it would be used by big recruiting customers, but soon after the launch we found that competing employment agencies wanted to use it. With some trepidation, we let them – it was our breakthrough.

Allowing direct competitors to advertise free on our site turned out to be one of the best marketing ploys ever used.

Over the next few years it made Reed's the first website candidates visited when looking for a job. True, they sometimes found jobs through other agencies, but the promotion of the Reed profile made it worth it.

Paul dreamed up the idea in 1999 and we launched in 2000 with a moody TV campaign, part of a £5 million investment. The ads showed various grainy scenarios set to sinister, suspense-ridden music as people searched for jobs. Suddenly an ad popped up in the most unlikely place. Then a voice asked, 'Why look for a job when the job can look for you? Go to reed.co.uk.'

I believe in the power of advertising, but it is no panacea. These were great advertisements and got us off to a high-profile start. Recruitment consultants who move around the various employment agencies also helped spread awareness by word of mouth. By 2000 we had 42,000 jobs being advertised on the site and doubled that in the next two years. When we hit 100,000 jobs for the first time, I took the team to lunch at the Ritz, something they remember very clearly – Martin still has the photograph of them all looking very young and happy.

By then, of course, all the employment agencies had websites, and the competition was hotting up. Martin and his team work hard to stay ahead of the game, constantly developing innovations for the site, which has now been through nine redesigns. One of the challenges of working online is that work is all too easy to copy or, to use the industry euphemism, 'be inspired by'.

Apart from the launch, we never gave reed.co.uk much of a marketing budget, so all the investment went on innovation; the search for new ideas has to be relentless. Martin tells me that if he puts something new on the site today one of our competitors could be copying it within two months. That means that as soon as we launch a new feature we need to be working on the next one.

Freecruitment was so successful as an idea that we gave Paul Rapacioli a bonus of £100,000 for thinking of it. I believe in rewarding individuals who really make a difference to the business, something I learned at Gillette. We gave him the money before the concept was a proven success because I am passionate about stimulating creativity and enterprise. At Reed we have a 'quick and dirty' ideas scheme called Reed Think, which provides a pool of cash for each operating company to reward staff for offering innovative ideas. We always give them the money before an idea is executed to show that we place value on sheer creativity. The scheme encourages enterprising behaviour throughout the organisation.

Sadly Paul stayed for only a further two years. He fell in love with and married Lotta from Sweden, where he created an English news website for ex-pats. It has been so successful that a lot of Swedes use it as well. He has a phenomenally creative brain.

We have continued to give incentives for innovative thought, and in 2011 we offered £50,000 for the best idea from our people.

As 'Founder at Large' I still keep an eye on all aspects of the business. Quite early on, reed.co.uk introduced a feature that allows users to point out errors or omissions, so every so often I look through the site; if I spot something – the wrong logo or a spelling mistake – I let them know. I also drop in to the office from time to time, but never tell them

I am coming. Martin has tried to persuade me to give him notice, but I want to see the office as it really is; I do not want them to make a special fuss.

James and Martin have a weekly meeting in the new office in Covent Garden. More than 120 people were working there by 2011 and the business was taking on seven or eight new staff every month. Hitwise, which monitors the sector regularly, says we are the market leader, but even so, because of the highly fragmented nature of the market, we can claim only about 5 per cent of the visitor traffic.

Hitwise figures at the end of 2010 showed our site had three million unique users a month, advertised more than 100,000 jobs across more than 40 sectors, and generated more than two million job applications a month. It is hard to know to what extent this cannibalises our bricks and mortar business, but as yet we have not noticed an appreciable drop in business through our branches.

There is still a lot to go for. About 5,000 internet sites advertising jobs, known as job boards, are aimed at the British market, but our main competitors are owned by publishers and newspaper groups who set up websites as their print advertising began to migrate to the internet. While we travelled from bricks and mortar, publishing businesses such as Reed Elsevier migrated from print. Reed Business Information (part of Reed Elsevier) owns Total Jobs, Associated Newspapers owns Jobsite, and the Monster board, which started in the US, has also grown strongly in Britain. Relations between the competitors have not always been good; we had a six-year battle with Reed Business Information, about which more later.

In 2007, seven years after we introduced Freecruitment,

we decided to restrict competitors to 50 ads each year and to charge for any above that total – it's called monetising the site.

Partly the advertisers were to blame; the site had got out of hand. Recruiters realised over time that if they posted a vacancy, because there was no payment control, it was easy to post the same one again or just leave the job up on the site. There were more than 300,000 ads sitting on the site, many of which were duplicates or way out of date. Some would stay on the site for as long as three months, so it was far more difficult for users to see which jobs really were available. We realised that it could lead to applicants deserting the site for our rivals'.

Urging recruiters to keep their listings tidy had only a limited effect, so Martin realised that a more drastic measure was required. We had to regulate by pricing. Martin and his team spent two months planning the changes, training the sales team, devising rate cards and working on the marketing. Even so, nothing had prepared them for the angry response they received on the morning they sent the email telling users that what had always been a free service was about to cost them.

Within minutes every phone started ringing with anguished calls. Martin remembers that several advertisers declared they would never use us again. 'It was astonishing,' he told me. 'Customers who had used us for several years and made hundreds of thousands of pounds from using our website declared that they would stop using us. One said he would never pay us a bean.'

But the people at reed.co.uk kept their cool. We knew we had already built a very strong brand and that the product was the best in the business. In response to threats to leave the site we replied that we would regretfully accept the decision. In time most advertisers recognised that by forcing people to be more disciplined, the service to applicants would be improved. We were also offering clients new services such as the ability to search the CV database and to use more visual campaigns on the website.

Within a couple of weeks everyone had calmed down, most users stayed with us and many more joined. In the end monetising the site was a huge success.

Like many young internet businesses, reed.co.uk makes only a small profit because we are still continuing to invest in it. James and I are always happy to let them try new things because that is the nature of the business. We have to have the best product online or else we cannot remain the market leader and eventually put ourselves in a position to make a larger profit.

* * *

One of our biggest battles was with Reed Elsevier, a multinational publishing and communications house specialising in business and science. For many years there had been some background confusion over our names, but the arrival of the internet made us head-on competitors. Reed Business Information, one of its divisions, owns 200 or so specialist magazines, a number of which carry job adverts.

Reed Elsevier soon realised that the only way to compete with internet job sites was to join them, and so it decided to set up a site called Totaljobs. I had been quite friendly with Peter Davis when he was chief executive, but he quit after the merger with Elsevier and I did not know his successor, Sir Crispin Davis.

The Totaljobs website had a similar design to that of reed.co.uk, but the real problem was the use of the Reed name on the site and the use of special search tags, which are technically known as metatags. Metatags are invisible to the user, but ensure that someone putting the name Reed into Google would find the Totaljobs website coming up very high up on the list of responses to a Reed search. It was the cyberspace equivalent of a supermarket switching every road sign pointing to a competitor's store towards its own premises.

We had registered Reed as our trademark for employment agency services from 1986 and felt that Reed Elsevier was infringing it. To the casual user looking for a job, the difference between the websites, we felt, was not immediately apparent.

Reed Elsevier is a huge multinational company compared with Reed Executive, and I felt that there was no need for this kind of behaviour, but my attempts at informal negotiations got nowhere. It was clear that no Reed Elsevier director was prepared to talk to me about it.

Recruitment is our entire business but carrying job adverts in their publications was just a sideline for Reed Elsevier so I felt very strongly about this. I did not feel inclined to be walked over by a publishing giant, and decided to sue for infringement of our trademark and for 'passing off'. I have been accused of enjoying litigation, and while it is true that I relish a good battle, it applies only when I am confident that I am in the right. I hate bullies and this case looked crystal clear to me.

We started proceedings in 2000 and the case finally came to court in 2002. Part of Reed Elsevier's defence was that it had always been in recruitment through job ads in its various publications.

I sat in the High Court throughout the hearing and was delighted when we won, and that appeared to be that. Afterwards I wrote to Sir Crispin Davis what I thought was a friendly, conciliatory letter, but received a very terse response that should have been a pointer to what happened next.

To my amazement, Reed Elsevier appealed against the judgment. Our legal team, headed by Joan Edmunds and advised by our QC, thought the appeal was unlikely to succeed. We had, however, reckoned without Lord Justice Jacob, who with two other appeal court judges, overturned the High Court's verdict, having taken the view that when the Totaljobs site came up in response to internet searches for Reed it was clear that it was not part of Reed Employment.

My understanding is that the appeal court believed the internet is difficult to control because there are no national boundaries and that restrictions would be anti-competitive. This was at odds with the view of our QC, one of the best brains on intellectual property in Britain. He believed, as did I, that our trademark was being infringed and that we had to act to protect our brand and our business.

There is now relative peace in terms of our UK business and I am pleased to say that if you search for Reed or Reed Employment our site pops up first; the Totaljobs website comes about tenth on the list. However, the war has now gone global. We have applied for Reed as a trademark for 'recruitment' in Europe and other international territories and most of these applications have been opposed by Reed Elsevier. Although our website generally covers applicants in the UK, our growth internationally means that we have to protect our name globally. The battle cost us around £5 million – expensive, but worth it.

* * *

In 2000, after three years of James and me working together – him as chief executive, but me still very much executive chairman – I decided that he had proved himself sufficiently for me to hand over more fully and become non-executive chairman. At that point, James, I believed, needed a younger group of people round him.

The early team – Mary Newham, who had started and grown our health division, Mike Whittaker, our property supremo, and me – were all heading for or had reached retirement age. I had set up generous pension schemes that allowed both Mary and Mike to retire at 60. When the time came, however, neither of them wanted to stop working! I found an inducement for Mary, who eventually retired in 1996, by giving her one of the Reed Health branches as her own private venture. Over the following few years she turned it into a successful niche business and sold it for more than £1 million – a nice little retirement cushion.

Mike, who has become one of my closest friends, posed another problem. By that time his work in seeking out new branches in the UK was virtually complete. The bricks and mortar employment agency market had become mature as long-term contracts and the web took over as engines of growth. Mike had stepped down from the board in 1997 and he finally retired from the company in 1999. Nowadays he helps me with my charitable endeavours, working from the Reed Foundation office two or three times a week. We often share a joke or two over lunch and a bottle of wine, and he takes numerous holidays with us. He trawls the newspapers every day and passes on relevant clippings, be they about charity, the latest technology or new trends in the recruitment industry. On Thursday evenings we often walk home together.

For Reed, the 1990s ended on a spectacular note. In 1999 our profits soared by 25 per cent to top £20 million before tax, a peak at the time, although in 2005 we were to make a record £35 million. I was particularly proud that our growth over nearly forty years had been purely organic – even our diversification into retail through Medicare had been organic. We had started from scratch and built up the chain gradually.

I was never infected by the merger mania of the 1980s. During the thirty years we were a public company it was a very important part of the strategy not to dilute the family's holding below a majority, so that we always had control. For me, ownership is all. We built Reed organically into the biggest employment agency brand in the country by doing things properly. Being an accountant, I have never confused size with value. Many companies merged just for the sake of merging, egged on by investment bankers looking for fees. I have enjoyed taking an increasing market share, but for me, if growth is not organic, it is not growth. There is no real growth in adding two and two to make four, or, as often happens in takeovers and mergers, less than four.

In my final chairman's statement before I became

non-executive I was able to reflect, 'From an initial investment of £75 when I first started the company and a valu-
ation on flotation of £1.5 million, the company is capital-
ised today at approximately £114 million, having returned
£15 million capital to shareholders on the sale of Medicare
in 1986.'

It was a good moment for me to relinquish executive
responsibility and become non-executive chairman.

CHAPTER 18

Publish and be damned: the *Mail on Sunday* and me

I T WAS A BEAUTIFUL EARLY SUMMER'S EVENING on Saturday 7 June 2003, but I remember that weekend as one of the worst of my life. While we were having supper, a thief entered my study in Little Compton and stole my laptop. The barking of our dogs did not alert us and it seemed the laptop was all that he wanted. In any case, although nobody was prosecuted, the evidence suggested that the thief had driven for an hour to travel 40 miles from Gloucester, where he lived, passing many villages like ours on the way.

The next morning the *Mail on Sunday* ran a front-page story about me. It covered the top half of the page, accompanied by a huge photograph of me. It was not complimentary. 'Blair donor in £3 million fraud raid' ran the banner headline. Whether the theft and the story were connected I shall never know. All I can say is that it seemed a remarkable coincidence to me.

I knew a story was coming, because James had told me on the Friday evening that the *Mail on Sunday* was doing a piece on Reed in Partnership in Liverpool. We were used to press coverage, which was generally complimentary or, at worst, neutral. I had assumed that it would be a positive article highlighting the work Reed was doing to ease the unemployment in economically stricken Liverpool. How wrong I was.

The story, written by Dominic Turnbull – I hope his mother is proud of him – who went on to become deputy news editor at the *Mail on Sunday*, was part of the paper's on-going campaign against the Labour government and anyone who gave it financial support. An equally damaging three-deck headline was splashed across the inside page: 'Police raid Labour donor over £3 million asylum fraud claims.' The headlines and the first two paragraphs of the story dramatically distorted and exaggerated my role in the investigation.

The first paragraph read: 'Labour faces a new sleaze scandal after police investigating a £3 million fraud involving illegal immigrants raided a top party donor's offices yesterday. The donor, Alec Reed, has given nearly £150,000 to Labour and is a business ally of Lord Sawyer, a former general secretary of the party.'

To the casual reader, both the headline and the first paragraph implied that my personal office had been raided, or at the very least, the head office in London. The round figure of £3 million seemed to be plucked out of the air, although I suspect it was the result of some back-of-the-envelope calculations made by the police on various assumptions.

It was not until the seventh paragraph on an inside page that the reader learned that the office raided was a Reed in Partnership branch in Liverpool, not, as the story insinuated, my personal office.

By that time, I had become non-executive chairman

of Reed and was spending an increasing proportion of my time working on the various charities within Reed Foundation, on my plans to convert an Ealing school into the West London Academy, and supporting the Labour Party. I had become close to Tom Sawyer, (now Lord) who was the party's General Secretary between 1994 and 1998. After he stood down, I asked him to become a non-executive director of Reed and later the chairman of Reed Health, which we spun off into a separate public company in 2001. He was still chairman in 2003.

Adrianne has always hated any kind of flamboyance that might attract attention. She once told me, albeit jokingly, that she would leave me if I ever bought a Rolls-Royce. Her antennae told her that making a donation of that size to the Labour Party was foolhardy. I knew from our conversations that she would disapprove and I held back from telling her about it until I had sent the cheque. When I did pluck up the courage to tell her, she was furious, warning me of the danger of putting my head above the parapet. How right she was.

In the spring of 2003 Associated Newspapers, which then owned the *Daily Mail*, the *Mail on Sunday* and the *Evening Standard*, was gunning for anyone supporting the Labour government, which by then was in its second term. Although the *Daily Mail* had carried a handful of complimentary articles about Tony Blair's early reforms after his victory in the 1997 election, it had soon reverted to its traditional pro-Conservative, anti-Labour stance. It has supported the Conservatives in every election since 1945.

The invasion of Iraq alongside the Americans in March of that year had made the government unpopular with large numbers of the British people. Associated Newspapers appeared to be against the invasion, and the editorial stance in its titles was highly critical of Tony Blair and anyone seen to be supporting him; if impropriety could be shown, so much the better.

Reed in Partnership was the Reed subsidiary that had worked under contract with the government's Action Team for Jobs programme since 2000. It was part of the Government's Welfare to Work programme through which Reed in Partnership had placed more than 120,000 people in jobs by 2010. The programme was designed specifically to help the long-term unemployed find permanent jobs, and under the contract Reed was also allowed to place asylum seekers as long as they could produce adequate paperwork showing their cases to be genuine.

Crucially, it was not part of Reed's remit to investigate whether documents were forgeries. If they appeared to be genuine, we passed the job seekers through to the next stage, in this case another agency called Monarch. Under its agreement with all the agencies it used, the Action Team for Jobs unit paid Reed in Partnership a fee for every person it placed in a job for three months or more. The *Mail on Sunday* said this was £2,000, but the figure was less than £1,000 per person, most of which was spent on preparing and training each candidate.

Unbeknown to James, the director of Reed in Partnership, its manager or me, the Liverpool branch of Reed in Partnership was under investigation by Merseyside Police as part of a wider-ranging probe into the placing of illegal immigrants with forged papers. Merseyside Police said that they had been working on the investigation for six months, but none of our staff had any inkling of this. Somehow the *Mail on Sunday* had found out about it.

Here the story becomes murky. According to police evidence, Merseyside Police were planning to ask for material from Reed's central office in Liverpool in mid-June. The plan was to do this in a low-key manner during working hours. But on 2 June a journalist at the *Mail on Sunday* contacted the Immigration Service, which passed the paper's inquiry to Merseyside Police. The journalist said that the *Mail on Sunday* was planning to run an article on Sunday 8 June revealing that such an investigation was taking place.

The police asked the paper to hold the story for a couple of weeks, but, as my journalist friends tell me, this is a very risky strategy for a newspaper with a big story. The police actually threatened the *Mail on Sunday* with an injunction, but the paper's lawyers responded by saying that it would require the police to give a cross-undertaking to the court to cover any loss the paper might suffer if the injunction was wrongly granted. The police decided that they did not wish to take that risk and instead brought forward the visit to Reed's offices to Saturday 7 June.

The *Mail on Sunday* called the visit a 'raid', as if the police had made a forced entry. In fact, they obtained search warrants and rang our manager at home so that he could open the premises for them. The police statement issued on Monday 9 June said that 'police officers met with members of staff at the property who assisted them in searching for files and documents relating to an immigration and fraud enquiry'. It went on to say: 'The fraud enquiry relates to a number of contracts valued at just under £3 million over a four year period.' (I still do not know how they came up with the figure of £3 million, but it looked good in a headline.)

The *Mail on Sunday*'s story used the word 'alleged' to protect itself from a possible libel suit in case of any inaccuracy. One sentence stated: 'It is alleged it flouted Government rules by placing illegal immigrants in jobs that should have gone to the unemployed.' A similar claim was made in the leader column. A police statement later denied the allegation.

The police statement was carefully worded. It read: 'The enquiry relates to illegal workers not entitled to work in the UK and documents that should be supplied when entering into employment ... Merseyside Police can confirm they are not investigating Reed in Partnership for *putting illegal workers into employment ahead of other unemployed people and that Mr Reed is not under investigation.*' (My italics.)

This final part of the statement, made almost as a throwaway line, was ignored by the *Mail on Sunday*, which resolutely refused to print a correction or an apology. Its in-house legal team, headed by Mary Russell, refused to acknowledge that there was any damage to me personally or that the way the story was written distorted the facts.

I was not only angry, I was hurt. I had a relationship with the *Daily Mail* going back to 1994, when I started to write regular articles for its Career Mail section. At one point the paper ran a piece on the mothers-in-law of high-flying men featuring James, his wife Nicola and Adrianne. There was a great picture of Adrianne and Nicola together looking the perfect mother and daughter-in-law.

So it was doubly hurtful that such a damaging article could appear out of the blue in the *Daily Mail*'s sister paper.

I could not understand how a journalist could write a story about an individual without first speaking to him to get his reaction. I did later discover that Mr Turnbull had put in a call to my London home on the Saturday night and left a message on the answering machine.

This is known as the 'right of reply' call made by journalists when reporting a revelatory story. I am told that such calls are often made as late as possible, thus giving little opportunity for the story to be denied or explained in a less sensationalist light. There is also the fear of an injunction being granted to prevent publication if the subject of such a story is alerted too soon.

If he had really wanted to track me down, Mr Turnbull could have done so through Reed's PR consultants, but clearly he believed his sources. Who they were I can only speculate, but it seems likely that they were close to the police or the Home Office or both.

The police investigation came to nothing. Although Chris Melvin, the chief executive of Reed in Partnership, told the *Mail on Sunday* that over the previous summer the firm had placed some illegal immigrants with forged papers, it was clear that it had not done so knowingly.

Chris was quoted in the *Mail* article as saying: 'Last summer there were a number of people with fraudulent paperwork which we were unable to detect.' Our Liverpool staff co-operated fully with the police investigation, which turned up nothing of a fraudulent nature on Reed's part.

Under the Labour government's Action Team for Jobs contract, Reed in Partnership was authorised to work with 'refugees and asylum seekers who are eligible for Government funded support'. The Department for Work and

Pensions made regular audits to ensure we were complying with Home Office guidelines on checking eligibility to work; that is, inspecting passports and papers. We conducted a thorough review of the process of supplying asylum seekers as workers to companies and uncovered problems in only a handful of cases. As I said, it is extremely difficult to detect forgeries.

The police continued to investigate our Liverpool office and insisted on interviewing some of our staff under caution at a police station. Nothing was achieved other than frightening and demoralising our staff. Over time, the police investigation melted away and we retained our Action Team for Jobs contract. No charges were ever brought against anyone at Reed in Partnership.

Miraculously, we did not lose a single client. The week after the article appeared, we wrote to every client assuring them that the story was a distortion of the facts and assuring them of our honesty in all our dealings.

The whole affair upset me more than anything else in my life other than the death of my parents. I have always prided myself on my integrity and the probity of the company and the way it conducts its affairs. We strive to operate to the highest standards and at times have been prepared to sacrifice short-term profits to maintain them. The whole episode challenged my ideas about justice.

But what upset me almost more than the story itself was the *Mail on Sunday*'s intransigence.

Through Joan Edmunds, our legal director, I contacted a QC who advised me that I had a 60:40 chance of successfully suing the paper. He also said I should use a different firm from our company lawyer. So I contacted Farrer & Co., in Lincoln's Inn Fields, which had been our family's firm of lawyers for some years, where I was directed to Julian Pike, an experienced media libel lawyer.

At our first meeting, he advised me that rather than issuing a writ immediately we should ask for an apology from the *Mail on Sunday* to be printed with reasonable prominence, plus a payment for the damage to my reputation to be paid to a charity of my choice. He seemed confident that we had a good chance of persuading the paper to run a correction and apology and suggested the following wording:

On the front page of the *Mail on Sunday* two weeks ago we led with an article entitled 'Blair Donor in £3m Fraud Raid'. The piece claimed that Mr Alec Reed, the founder of the Reed Employment agency and a donor to the Labour Party, had his office raided by the police investigating a £3 million fraud on the taxpayer. We very much regret that this claim was wrong.

We wish to put the record straight by making it clear that Mr Reed's office, which is in London, was not raided by the police. We also confirm that Mr Reed is not, as has been confirmed by the police, the subject of any investigation whether into an alleged £3 million fraud or otherwise.

For reasons I find hard to fathom, the *Mail on Sunday* resolutely refused to admit that there had been anything misleading about its story and refused to print the correction and apology.

Early on, a senior police officer told Julian Pike over the telephone that the police would be prepared to testify as to the behaviour of the *Mail on Sunday* when officers threatened an injunction. The officer also said the police would prepare a complaint to the Press Complaints Commission. However, as the prospect of a court hearing drew nearer, the police decided against supporting my case and did not complain formally to the PCC.

Nevertheless, I felt sure that the PCC would uphold my complaint. I am afraid I ignored Julian Pike's advice that 'it would be a waste of time'. His experience was that the PCC rarely upheld complaints when there was dispute over the facts.

However, I was full of zeal and felt passionately that right was on my side. So at my behest, on 10 July Julian Pike wrote to the Press Complaints Commission setting out the case. After more than a month, on 11 August, he was proved right when we received a lengthy letter from the commission explaining why it had refused to uphold our complaint.

I was outraged, and my instinct was to pursue the *Mail on Sunday* in the courts. But in the weeks prior to the article appearing, a small lump on my head had been growing, and by July my forehead had begun to swell into what I dubbed my 'unicorn look'. Tests revealed my worst fears. The growth was cancerous.

The growth was unconnected to my previous cancer; this time it was non Hodgkins lymphoma.The lymphoma was removed, this time at the London Clinic followed by a course of chemotherapy. The scar is still obvious, and although I was having the lump investigated before the article appeared, I call it 'my Mail on Sunday headline'. Again, I am lucky that the cancer is in remission. I could

Adrianne receives my unusual anniversary present at Little Compton, September 1980

Me (at right) with my elder brother John at his son Tom's wedding in France, 31 August 1991

HRH Diana, Princess of Wales, and me at a Mother's Day charity lunch that I hosted at the London Marriott Hotel, Grosvenor Square, on 8 March 1991 in support of the National Foster Care Association and the Thomas Coram Foundation

With Tony Blair, daughter-in-law Nicola (wife of my son James), and Adrianne at the Labour Party annual dinner at the Hilton, Park Lane, in 1997

With James (at left), celebrating Kate Pigott's birthday in 2004. Kate was Reed's longest-serving temp – she had been with the company for 36 years

Darby and Joan, 2000

Me with grandchildren Aidan and Hazel by the Wendy house at Little Compton, spring 2001

At a party for employees' families at Little Compton. I have always liked the straightforwardness of children

My family: Adrianne, our children, their spouses and our eleven grandchildren at a family party at Little Compton in May 2007

I took up painting with enthusiasm late in life. I was amazed when *Nice Hat* won the Over 60s Art Award in July 2003

Ben and me enjoying each other's company at Little Compton in 2010

Opening a Cheshire care centre in Addis Ababa during my
October 2010 visit with my daughter Alex to Ethiopia

How to stand out in a crowd! Among enthusiastic spectators at
a variety show organised by a local partner of the the charity
Ethiopiaid to highlight poor treatment of women in October
2010

Martyn Lewis and Dame Stephanie Shirley presenting me with the Beacon Award for philanthropy in November 2010

With Gemma Bond, then First Artist of the Royal Ballet, at their Covent Garden rehearsal rooms in 2007. The photo was taken to accompany an article about The Big Give in a charity magazine

Receiving my knighthood from HRH Prince Charles at Buckingham Palace on 8 February 2011

Outside Buckingham Palace: the proud father with (from left) James, Lady Reed, Alex and Richard

have then sued the *Mail on Sunday* for libel, but the police change of heart about giving evidence and the response of the Press Complaints Commission did not augur well. Julian Pike also advised me that if we sued and I died prior to the case being concluded, my estate would be liable for substantial costs – up to £2 million – incurred by both sides. Apart from the possibility of leaving my family with a huge financial burden, there was the emotional distress to consider. Adrianne was adamant; if I was ill already, surely the strain of a drawn-out court case would only damage my chances of recovery. So I backed off, albeit reluctantly. Only in 2010, seven years later, did we receive complete formal clearance from the police.

I was so injured by the events that soon after, in 2003, I resigned as non-executive chairman of Reed, leaving James as chairman and chief executive. Rather than being called President like some retired founders, I coined the title Founder at Large, which suits me very well.

The whole episode soured my view of the press in general and of Associated Newspapers in particular. To this day I refuse to let a copy of either the *Daily Mail* or the *Mail on Sunday* enter my house or my office.

CHAPTER 19

Back to school

I N 1999, ADRIANNE AND I DECIDED TO 'RETIRE' to London and moved from Englefield Green to Kensington. We had the pleasure of the countryside at Little Compton at the weekends, and any rationale for living in a small village near Windsor during the week had long ceased. We both enjoy the cultural wealth of London – the theatre, opera and great exhibitions as well as being close to our London friends. For Adrianne, who had given up her work with the Trustees Register, it was important to have her interests close by. She belongs to several groups that take an interest in the arts, and driving back to Englefield Green after a night out is no fun. We also felt that, as we grew older, it was good to have the resources of central London at our disposal.

My involvement with Royal Holloway lasted from 1979, and I still have an occasional role. I had taught the LIES course for six years, and I decided that as I was moving to London, I would stop teaching. I looked around for new areas of charitable work. During the early 1990s I had been beguiled, like many before me, into the sponsorship of secondary education by Sir Cyril Taylor, the pioneer of the

Academy specialist schools, part funded by philanthropic businessmen. In the late 1990s he invited me to a dinner at what was then the ADT Technology College in Wandsworth, founded by Michael (now Lord) Ashcroft, who is never out of the news for long. It was subsequently renamed the Ashcroft Technology Academy under the Labour government's Academy programme.

Sir Cyril is a remarkable man. He had the ear of three prime ministers, Margaret Thatcher, John Major and Tony Blair, and advised five education secretaries from differing political parties, persuading them to back a programme of sponsoring specialist schools. Originally they were called City Technology Colleges, then City Academies, but the Labour government dropped the 'City'. As time went by, Sir Cyril was able to show that the pupils attending technology colleges achieved greatly improved GCSE results. He was therefore listened to closely by the various education secretaries, from Kenneth Baker in 1987 to Alan Johnson in 2007, when he stepped down.

My fellow dinner guests were all successful entrepreneurs who, like me, were keen to hear about Thatcher's Academy programme. A born salesman who started his career at Procter & Gamble, Sir Cyril headed the Specialist Schools and Academies Trust for twenty years. That evening he made a compelling speech explaining the benefits to children and the surrounding areas from City Academies. He also spelled out what someone needed to do to sponsor a City Academy, what they needed to spend and what they might get out of it in terms of fulfilment and recognition.

Sir Cyril's speech caught my imagination. Despite my own difficult experiences as a schoolboy, I know that education is one of the most important gifts, next to confidence, that you can give a child. Far too many of our young people leave school barely able to read and write; many do not possess useful skills to help them earn a living. I also believe that school should be a place where children have fun while their brains are stimulated; it should not just be endured. Children are the consumers of education and therefore the product needs to be made attractive so that they want to 'buy' it.

At that time a donor had to give £1 million towards the cost of setting up a City Academy in return for his name in lights and considerable involvement in the way the school was run. I liked the idea of improving the lot of pupils in the area where I went to school, and decided to find a school in Ealing. Soon after that dinner, though, Margaret Thatcher went cold on the idea and halted the programme. John Major's government revived it, but it was not until New Labour was elected that I became involved again.

Despite Sir Cyril's closeness to the Conservatives, when Labour won the 1997 election he sold the idea to Tony Blair, who loved it because it fitted so well with his mantra of 'Education, Education, Education'. Although he repackaged the scheme, the main change was the price – Labour put up the required donation to £2 million and changed the name. Blair called the new schools simply Academies rather than City Academies.

I was keener than ever to sponsor a school now that the Conservatives had gone, and I had thrown my hat in with the new government.

As a newcomer to the Academy world, I decided to undertake some research. I hosted a lunch at the fish restaurant Manzi's, now sadly closed, and invited various people who had already sponsored an Academy. Only five accepted, but we had a very useful discussion. Frank Lowe, the founder of the advertising agency Lowe Howard-Spink, later sold to Interpublic, was there, along with the property developer Sir David Garrard, a larger-than-life character who, like me, had switched from supporting the Conservatives to Labour. He had flown in especially on his private jet from the Cipriani in Venice. The late Sir Clive Bourne, who was well known for his philanthropic work, also attended, so it was quite a jolly lunch.

As an aside, Sir David, who was going back to the airport, offered me a lift in his new Rolls-Royce to James's office where I had a meeting. Inside the car was a beautiful drinks cabinet alongside a TV screen. To my amusement, when he was showing me how it all worked, one of the straps fell off. He was furious, understandably.

In 2002 I decided to sponsor Compton High School in Ealing, renaming it the West London Academy. We also merged it with the Northolt Primary School so that it would take pupils right through from the reception year when they are four to A-levels at 18. It was a difficult challenge from the start. To my mind primary school culture is 'gold stars', whereas secondary schools are about detention. To complicate matters, the plan also included a special needs school that was to remain under local authority management. It was to be an interesting lesson in what happens when private-sector culture meets state-funded culture.

I had tremendous freedom in setting up the Academy. It was down to me to decide the school's aims and ethos, choose its head and commission the design of the buildings.

I went for what I thought was the safe option by appointing Foster & Partners, founded by the legendary Lord (Norman) Foster, to design the building. The designer of the 'Gherkin' Swiss Re building in the City of London as well as international projects such as the Chek Lap Kok airport in Hong Kong, Foster is one of the best-known architects in the world.

Intriguingly we had our problems along the way, because although Foster & Partners had built Sir David Garrard's Academy, the practice was more used to designing offices, but the end result is stunning – a quarter-mile-long two-storey building in mainly wood and glass so that light pours in. Sir Cyril Taylor was kind enough to say that our school should be the model for all future Academies. In the event, I contributed £2.5 million to a total cost of £40 million.

I chose Alastair Falk to be West London Academy's first head. When I advertised the job in the *Guardian* and on reed. co.uk I received a good response, and interviewed a handful of candidates. I narrowed the field to three who I asked to work on curriculum plans.

Although he was perhaps not the obvious choice, I chose Alastair because I liked the way he thought. At the time he was head of King Solomon High School in East London, a state-funded Jewish school. I am not in favour of faith schools because I feel they can be divisive in a world in which it is imperative that people of all religions and races live peaceably together. However, King Solomon High had achieved impressive improvements under Alastair's headship and, most important, I liked him.

I found him open-minded and his thinking was in tune

with mine. For instance, when I suggested that, instead of the pupils moving between classrooms for every lesson (which any teacher will tell you takes at least ten minutes from the allotted time), the teachers should switch classrooms, he thought it was a great idea; none of the other candidates could contemplate such a big change in the status quo. In retrospect, maybe they were right as the existing staff could not get their heads round it at all and it never happened.

I believed in paying well, advertising the post on a salary of more than £100,000 a year, well above the average for head teachers at the time, although by 2010 that was quite modest. Naïvely, I published the figure. When the press got hold of the story, there was quite a furore, which did not help Alastair's relations with his staff, who were paid a lot less. The *Times Educational Supplement* calculated that the average pay for a head in a state school at the time was £48,000, although other high-performing heads were earning nearer £100,000.

Alastair and I both underestimated the difficulties of trying to weld existing schools together as an Academy. Many of the staff who remained did not take kindly to a privately funded, highly paid head coming in and trying to change the way they did things. Alastair believed I had visionary educational ideas; others were not so sure. With hindsight, Alastair says he should have gone in with a small team of new teachers around him.

He worked closely with me on planning the Academy, and liked my unorthodox methods. I remember when we were talking about ordering school chairs – about 800 of them. The public-sector procurement chap was very pleased as he had found suitable chairs at £65 each when the official budget was £87. I told him he had to think of the chairs as a commodity and scour the world for the cheapest supplier. He was very reluctant to do so, saying he had already agreed the price with a supplier. I told him we had to find something better and eventually we found a company in Eastern Europe that was happy to supply them for about 40 per cent less.

I did not want the public areas of my Academy to look conventional. So I brought in a series of young, funky designers and told them to come up with something different. They certainly did. One wanted to instal a fairground, while another wanted to build an indoor garden in the special school. Some of the ideas were impractical, but we used a couple of them and it was good to see creativity at work.

Such cosmetic changes paled against the challenge of improving the school's results. It is in a deprived area, and many of the pupils come from poor immigrant families. The first Ofsted report in 2005 highlighted the incredible challenges Alastair and his staff were facing. Out of the 746 pupils in the secondary school, half were from minority ethnic groups, more than half of those spoke languages other than English at home, 45 per cent were entitled to free school meals and 27 per cent had special educational needs.

That report was quite critical, although there were some positive comments. The pupils themselves said they believed there had been an improvement. The inspectors, however, had misgivings about Alastair's style. He was quite radical with his policy of excluding disruptive students, because he felt that they hampered the chances of the other pupils.

Ofsted criticised him for the high rate of exclusions. In the year of the report there had been 265 fixed-term exclusions, more than treble the number in the previous year, and 20 pupils had been excluded permanently. Alastair pointed out that most parents supported the exclusion of disruptive and threatening students. 'The government can't have it both ways,' he told the inspectors. 'It preaches zero tolerance, but then we are rebuked for exclusions.'

I also provoked some criticism because I voiced two theories not popular with the educational establishment. The first was that we should drop the teaching of foreign languages. It seemed to me that in a school where half the pupils were struggling to learn English, attempting to make them learn French, German or Spanish was a waste of teaching resources. And half the world speaks English these days.

The second heap of criticism came down on me because of my decision not to have a library in the Academy, because the money could be better deployed. Children look up everything on the internet these days, and why not? I know of schools where the library is virtually unused.

Alastair did a lot of tough groundwork, but a combination of staff intransigence, the problems with the state-run special needs school and negative Ofsted reports resulted in him leaving in 2005 after only two years. He came to me and said, 'Mr Reed, I feel my position is untenable.' It was particularly sad because the pupils had not then even moved into the new buildings; when they did, it made a huge difference to morale.

A first head leaving a new Academy was not unusual. Of the twelve Academies set up in the early part of this century, eight of the heads left after two or three years, and many fell out with their sponsors. Luckily, that did not happen with Alastair and me.

West London Academy is not without challenges under its current head, Hilary Macaulay, who has done great work and it has received a wide range of awards. In 2010 the school received the Inclusion Quality Mark award, which recognises how schools see differences as opportunities for learning. It recognises how a school values diversity and how inclusive it is.

The high proportion of minority groups and the poverty of some of the families have not changed. Half the children are classified as having special educational needs. An Academy's success should be measured not by its overall results, but by the value it adds; in other words, how much does an Academy improve the children's results compared with what they would have achieved in the old school? That is the crucial thing. There is a way to estimate a child's potential and then measure how much the school adds to that. My school is fantastic for adding value, one of the best in England, even though the overall results are still not as good as we would like.

The latest Ofsted report in 2010 gave the school a mark of 2 – equivalent to good for overall effectiveness – and the inspectors made many positive comments about the teaching and general ethos. Even so the number of children attaining GCSE in maths, science and English remains below the national average although it is improving.

Part of my legacy is that the school has specialist status for sports and enterprise.

That part of Ealing has a high percentage of Indian,

Pakistani and Polish families, most of whom speak English as a second language. Yet once these children become fluent in English, many of them outperform the indigenous population by a mile. Their parents are very strict, make sure they do their homework and are delighted when they do well. I still keep in contact with the school and it has three Reed trustees. Derek Beal, the school's chairman, is Reed's finance director.

When Alastair quit I suppose I could have blamed him, but I admired his keen intellect and his passion for education. I asked him to join my Academy of Enterprise, which I set up to promote enterprise in schools. Some schools wanted to achieve specialist status and we helped about thirty of them through the application process, spending around £500,000.

I had long dreamed of creating a GCSE in Enterprise, but I did not really know how to go about it until Alastair came along. He was somewhat fazed when I said I wanted it within nine months, because a new GCSE course normally takes two years to develop. But I must have galvanised him into action because, sure enough, after nine months he had produced a GCSE course on Enterprise and won approval for it from the Department of Education. In addition, during his first year, he created a substantial network of schools in the poorest areas such as Tower Hamlets that we re-energised and repositioned. Together I believe we earned the respect of the Department of Education. I told him we should always punch above our weight and never waste public money. In fact, I felt it was our duty to make it go as far as it could.

Alastair says I became his mentor. I don't know about that, but it is true I advised him to give up teaching because

I felt his talents were much broader-based. After a couple of years at the Academy of Enterprise he applied for and won a strategic role advising on education and leadership with all the Jewish schools across the country. He and I disagreed about faith schools, but we agreed on enough other things to get on well.

* * *

My other direct investment in education came about many years earlier when I bought the estate at Little Compton. The land was graced by a breathtaking Jacobean manor house where William Juxon, King Charles I's chaplain and one of his bishops, lived after the king was executed. Although the house is beautiful, it was too big for a family home. I have never wanted to live in a grand house – something some fellow entrepreneurs find strange. Instead, as I mentioned earlier, I turned it into the Reed Business School and converted three gardeners' cottages on the estate into our comfortable family home.

The oldest parts of the manor date back to the fifteenth century; it has an intriguing history. In the timbered dining room hangs a portrait of Juxon, whose brother Thomas left him the estate in 1644. William was then the Bishop of London and under King Charles I he became Lord High Treasurer of England, the first bishop to hold that post. Juxon also sat on the King's Council and advised Charles during the Civil War. Juxon voluntarily surrendered to arrest with King Charles and shared his captivity.

When the king was executed in January 1649, Juxon was the only person to accompany him to the scaffold, where he offered him the last rites. The king was beheaded, but at Windsor his head was sewn back on to his corpse to enable him, as they thought at the time, to enter heaven intact. His body was embalmed under Juxon's directions, and Juxon then took the coffin to St George's Chapel in Windsor Castle. These scenes are depicted in a stained-glass window in the church at Little Compton.

Later in 1649, Juxon was forced to give up his bishopric and was exiled to Little Compton, where he indulged his great love of deer hunting. We still keep fallow deer in the former deer park, which is one of the smallest in Britain. Deer hunting was banned by the Roundheads, but when some busybody told Oliver Cromwell that Juxon was hunting, he reportedly said, 'Well, if that's all Juxon is up to we should leave him alone.'

When Charles II became king in the Restoration, he made Juxon Archbishop of Canterbury. Juxon died in 1663, leaving £100 to the poor of the parish; his coat of arms is set above the fireplace in the manor.

Our business school offers various accountancy courses. It has been ably run by Stella Shaw since 1991; she has three full-time tutors, numerous part-time teachers and an administrative team supporting her. There is also a team of gardeners.

The Reed Business School is run on a not-for-profit basis and it is owned by the Reed Educational Trust. Some of our staff do their training here and our pass rates are often close to 100 per cent and usually well above the national average. For example, in 2010 students studying for the Institute of Chartered Accountants in England and Wales (ICAEW) exam achieved 100 per cent passes in some papers. Overall our students achieved 92 per cent compared with the national average of 78 per cent. In financial reporting, 71 per cent of our students passed, slightly below a national average of 75 per cent.

But it is not all work and no play. One day a staff member was showing a group of potential delegates round the school when she approached the accommodation. 'This is a typical bedroom,' he announced, opening the door to reveal a couple having a romp on one of the beds. What he said next is not recorded, but no doubt he shut the door very quickly.

In the grounds are a tennis court, a volleyball court and an outdoor swimming pool for the sporty. The gardeners have created a world-class garden, which is beautifully kept to provide a peaceful environment conducive to study, friendship and sometimes even romance.

* * *

In my book *Capitalism Is Dead, Peoplism Rules*, I promote the idea of Unique Strategic Positioning. Put simply it means a strategy that uses the unique positioning of a company to increase revenue. That idea has been put into practice at Reed Learning, our training company based in Holborn. Reed Learning runs more than 250 non-residential courses for people wanting to improve their skills to make them more employable. Individuals are welcome, but most candidates are sent by companies which pay for their staff to hone their skills. This helps us to build contacts with big employers and raise their awareness of Reed.

Each quarter we send the brochure to more than

500,000 companies. Even if there is a poor take-up of the courses due to recession or tight budgets, the exercise raises awareness of the Reed group and our expertise in all areas of recruitment.

On the inside cover of each brochure is a letter from me telling potential candidates 'You can go anywhere from here,' and outlining some of our new courses, such as Sales for Non-Sales People, and Developing Team Performance. We also offer psychometric testing and a feedback report for employers. Reed Learning stems directly from my theory that the future belongs to the intelligent and skilled irrespective of race or gender. Unlike Reed Business School, Reed Learning is part of the Reed group and contributes to profits.

CHAPTER 20

Getting arty

APART FROM MY THREE-WEEK COURSE at Harvard, most of my further education has been self administered. However, I owe a lot of my knowledge of the arts to Adrianne. Gradually in our life together Adrianne has exposed me to new experiences and, although we have different preferences, I now enjoy music, ballet and art in a way I never would have without her.

When I stepped back from the business, I decided to start painting again. Adrianne wisely said: 'What you need is some lessons.' I agreed, so she found Ken Payne, a leading portrait painter, as that was what interested me. I became very keen and for a while I painted every day. It particularly helped me get through chemotherapy after my second run-in with cancer. I enjoy portraiture more than anything and to my amazement I won a national competition for the over-sixties for a self portrait in which I am wearing a trilby. It is called *The Hat*. The prize was presented to me at the House of Lords.

When we moved to London, I attended the Heatherly School of Fine Art's 'open studio' classes, where they give you access to paints and a model. My friend the Revd John Record, who was the vicar at Little Compton, came with me for a while after he moved to a parish in Hammersmith.

I enjoy art, but ballet is my passion. Ever since Adrianne introduced me to it, I have attended as many performances as time allows and became a donor to the Royal Ballet. But after a while, I wanted to do something more creative and become more involved with the Royal Opera House (ROH) other than just giving money.

So a few years ago, I approached Amanda Saunders, the Royal Opera House's Director of Development, and told her that I would be interested in sponsoring a new modern ballet. She introduced me to the formidable Monica Mason, then the 'Queen' of ballet at the ROH. I told her I wanted to help fund a contemporary family ballet – an alternative to the regular Christmas production of The *Nutcracker* – to which I could take all my grandchildren.

Her response was disappointing. 'Not in my lifetime,' she said. She explained that because the ROH is constantly on the edge financially, it was vital for each production to fill the auditorium. In other words, she was simply not prepared to take a risk with a new, unproven work. Until recently, the only time the Royal Opera House had put on a new ballet production was as part of a triple bill – when it could be sandwiched in between two well-known ballets.

However, it seems that I at least planted the seed of an idea, because in the spring of 2011 the Royal Opera House launched an extraordinary new full-length ballet of *Alice in Wonderland*, created by Christopher Wheeldon and composed by Joby Talbot. It went down a storm with the audiences, even though some of the critics were lukewarm.

There is no doubt it will become part of the Royal Ballet's repertoire for years to come.

Despite Monica Mason's disappointing response to me, I felt that the fund-raising team at the Royal Opera House was so dedicated that after that formal meeting I wrote a cheque for £100,000 over coffee. Monica and her team seemed absolutely amazed. Had she agreed to my proposal it would have been a lot more but I have carried on supporting the ROH as well as taking my grandchildren to their productions.

Despite that particular disappointment, I still wanted to be involved in a new and contemporary ballet, and when I was talking to Jon Brooks at the Reed Foundation one day he came up with a brilliant suggestion. 'Why don't you approach Matthew Bourne?' Bourne made his name sensationally in 1995 with what became known as 'the male Swan Lake'. The ballet met with immediate, almost hysterical acclaim. It was a bold move to recast the principal characters as men, with only the Queen being danced by a ballerina. It was first performed at the Edinburgh Festival, and since then the Bourne Swan Lake has toured the world, has won more than thirty international awards, and is performed regularly at Sadler's Wells.

In the mid 2000s, Matthew Bourne was working with Robert Noble, one of Sir Cameron Mackintosh's team, who was allowed also to work with Matthew. I met Robert at a meeting at Sir Cameron's offices and discovered that Matthew and he were very keen to obtain backing.

Matthew said they needed investors for a new version of Prokofiev's Cinderella, to be staged at Sadler's Wells at Christmas 2010. Before that they were close to staging a contemporary ballet based around Oscar Wilde's *Picture of Dorian Gray*. I really liked that idea and they agreed that I could invest in that as well as in *Cinderella*.

When it came to signing over money, however, they said they really did not need any more funding for *Dorian Gray*. Intuitively I knew the production would catch the public's imagination, so I protested that we had made a deal and they should stick to it, which they did. I am glad that I was firm, because I made 50 per cent profit and thus I was delighted to invest much more in *Cinderella*. The competition was stiff, though, because there were four versions of *Cinderella* at Christmas 2010.

Bourne's production turns Cinderella's Prince into a wounded RAF pilot. The ballet is danced among spectacular wartime sets, including the ballroom at the Cafe de Paris which suffered a direct hit during the Blitz. The Fairy Godmother becomes a striking male guardian Angel in a silver suit (danced stylishly by Christopher Marney), while the vampish Wicked Stepmother (danced by Michela Meazza) dominates the stage whenever she is on it. The show played at Sadler's Wells to full houses – and had great, if occasionally mixed reviews. I feel sure it will become a Christmas staple. I was proud to be an investor in such an original production and I made a good return on my investment.

Giving money to the arts is a lottery, but I like to say that if a show makes money it is an investment; if it is a flop then the money becomes a donation.

Although Sadler's Wells has made a name for itself as a venue for both ballet and other dance, the location is inconvenient, and I would like to see a theatre dedicated to ballet located more centrally in London. At the Royal Opera

House, ballet will always be viewed as the poor relation of opera, so if I had my way, I would put the Royal Ballet into the Coliseum in St Martin's Lane and leave Covent Garden to opera. However, that is probably a pipe dream.

In retrospect, I am glad Monica turned me down, because I have enjoyed being involved with Matthew Bourne. He is surprisingly down to earth for such a creative genius. He invites me to attend rehearsals and meet the dancers. That gives me a fascinating glance behind the scenes and is a real pleasure. I am happy to learn from anyone, whatever their age. That is why, at the Reed Foundation, I surround myself with young graduates who bounce their ideas off me, and each other, to great effect.

CHAPTER 21

Operation Starburst

IN MAY 2000 WE THREW A HUGE PARTY at the London Arena in Docklands to celebrate the company's 40th anniversary. I had passed my 66th birthday and James wanted me to celebrate the anniversary with a bang. The dotcom bubble was yet to burst, and the word in the City was that 'a new paradigm' had been achieved. We were in a Goldilocks economy – 'not too hot and not too cold' – in which the deluded believed there would never again be a crash. Later that year, at the Labour Party conference, Gordon Brown, then the Chancellor, made his famous declaration: 'We will not put hard-won economic stability at risk. No return to short-termism. No return to Tory boom and bust.' I like Gordon Brown, but he made himself a hostage to fortune with that speech.

Disaster lay around the corner, but meanwhile it seemed a good idea to hold a big party. We invited every co-member from around the country and as they arrived, bands played and actors in fancy dress welcomed them. It was very upbeat.

We kicked off in the morning with a presentation by James, after which I introduced a video on Ethiopiaid. I remember walking on to the stage to a rapturous reception which moved me greatly. I never speak from notes because I come alive in front of an audience and I gave them the most appreciative speech I could muster with a few jokes thrown in. My friend Lord (Tom) Sawyer says that I have the ability to make everyone in the company feel that I know them personally.

We enjoyed a big lunch, followed by a 'Stars in Their Eyes' competition in which various colleagues sang and performed other entertainments. There was a panel of judges and the audience voted for their favourites – it was corporate X-Factor.

After the winners were announced to rapturous applause we cruised up the Thames, drinking and dancing – it got quite wild. It was a beautiful evening, and I remember standing on deck counting my blessings while watching a spectacular sunset over Tower Bridge as it opened. Halcyon days compared with what was to follow.

* * *

Mary Newham had built Reed Health into a highly successful company within Reed Executive. When she retired in 1998, we passed her particular baton at Reed Health to Christa Echtle, her number two, who seemed eminently capable. Christa, who was German by birth and upbringing, had joined Reed around 1990, working mainly in the social care division of Reed Health. She had an MA in psychology and an MBA. Mary had found her well-organised and efficient, but felt that she lacked creativity. She was wrong about that.

The frenzied excitement of the dotcom bubble burst in

late 2000 and sent the stock market tumbling. By September 2000, Reed Executive's shares had slumped to below 70p and were trading on a lowly price/earnings multiple of between six and eight.

That troubled James more than me. As a young chief executive, naturally he wanted to create more value. He had the idea that if we turned the various divisions into separate companies within Reed Executive, then the sum of those parts would exceed that of the whole; he believed that some of them would be suitable to spin off as public companies. He worked hard on this strategy, naming it 'Starburst'. It sounded great to me; I had put my faith in James and I was keen for him to develop his own ideas.

Reed Health Group was the obvious candidate to be first out of the door. The recruitment groups specialising in health, in particular Nestor Healthcare, traded on much higher ratings than Reed Executive, so spinning it off as a public company was surely the logical thing to do.

Mary had run Reed Health as an autonomous unit with three divisions – Reed Social Care, which provided professionals in childcare, mental health and in caring for the elderly; Reed Nurse, which provided nurses, mainly to NHS Trusts; and Reed Health Professionals, which provided a range of temporary pharmacists, optometrists, laboratory technicians and so on.

By 2000, Christa had helped Mary to build Reed Health into a decent-sized company, making profits of £4.7 million on turnover of £57 million, so we felt that spinning it off on to the stock market would not be too complicated. Christa liked the idea of being the chief executive of a public company and owning shares; with hindsight I feel she liked the idea a little too much. Neither James nor I had realised how ambitious she was.

We floated Reed Health Group in June 2001 via an 'introduction of shares to the Official List' – cheaper and easier than a full flotation. Stock Exchange regulations forbade Reed Executive to hold shares in Reed Health, but as a family we held more than 60 per cent. James and Derek Beal became non-executive directors, while Tom Sawyer took on the chairmanship.

The float went swimmingly. Investors lapped up the shares and two well-known fund managers, Andy Brough at Schroder and Tim Steer at New Star, took sizeable chunks of the equity on offer.

The shares soon soared above the issue price and for a while the stock market value of Reed Health even exceeded that of Reed Executive. All seemed set fair. Christa, however, soon fell out with Malcolm Paget, her finance director, and replaced him with Desmond Doyle.

Desmond was more ambitious than Malcolm, and advised by James Wellesley Wesley at Granville Baird, the boutique investment bank that had sponsored the listing, the two of them were soon planning how to grow the company. James Wellesley Wesley is descended from the 1st Duke of Wellington, and he had made his reputation in the recruitment sector by selling Select Group, the company founded by my old managing director Romney Rawes, for a rather rich price. At least, that is my opinion.

Wellesley Wesley appeared to feel that Christa, who had no previous experience of the City, was someone he could guide to build the company through acquisitions. They did not waste much time.

In May 2002, less than a year after going public, Reed Health announced the acquisition of the Locum Group, a company specialising in supplying temporary medical staff, from doctors to laboratory technicians. It seemed a sensible acquisition. Instinctively I do not like acquisitions, but by that time I was standing well back in the wings.

They used a mixture of cash and shares to pay a high price for Locum, and the deal sounded the warning bell. The Reed family suddenly found its shareholding in Reed Health diluted to 55 per cent.

Christa's triumphalist tones in her letter to shareholders announcing the completion of the deal added to my unease. 'Under the new company, we have the exciting and quite genuine opportunity to build something special together!' she wrote, pointing out that the combined group was now the third largest in the health sector behind Nestor and Match Healthcare Services. She continued: 'I believe that with the strength, drive, intelligence and vision of the enlarged group we have the possibility of becoming a true market leader.'

That was all rather headier than James or I had intended. I had seen too many companies grow at breakneck speed, buying other businesses for shares, only to see them implode. James, Derek Beal (who was also a director) and Tom Sawyer found themselves in a difficult position. As directors of Reed Health Group they were bound by confidentiality rules not to talk to me about what went on at board meetings. James told me later that it had slowly dawned on them that Christa and Desmond had a more ambitious agenda than laid out at the time of the flotation.

I also began to hear feedback from suppliers that Christa

and Desmond were not happy about the family ties. Buoyed up by their success and the flattery of City analysts and advisors, it seemed to me that they had started to believe they were a better company than Reed Executive. From what I heard from outsiders, I felt there was some subtle undermining of James and me taking place.

Christa, Desmond and James Wellesley Wesley carried on making plans for more acquisitions. But they soon realised that having to seek shareholder approval every time was irksome. Why not obtain blanket permission from shareholders to make acquisitions, rather than have to obtain their agreement for each one? First, though, they had to put that plan forward as a resolution at the Annual General Meeting.

One crisp autumn morning, shortly before the AGM, I received the notice of the meeting. When I read the agenda I could barely believe my eyes. There, in black and white, was a resolution that proposed depriving shareholders of the right to vote on acquisitions. In other words, Christa and Co. could make acquisitions below a certain size using the company shares without consulting us. That meant the Reed family's shareholding could easily be diluted below the level at which we had a majority. In one fell swoop we would lose control of the company. That was something that neither James nor I had foreseen.

I knew that to keep control I had to act fast, and act alone. Over the next few days I collected all the family proxies, and those of other loyal shareholders and deposited them with the registrar. The only proxies I did not collect were James's.

On the morning of the meeting on 26 November, I rang Mike Whittaker, feeling nervous. 'Come to Reed Health's

AGM and give me some moral support,' I said. Mike did not need asking twice, so we met and went to Granville Baird's offices in the City where the meeting was being held.

The annual meeting was expected to be a routine affair; no press attended and there were not that many shareholders. The board may have got wind that I was not happy with the resolutions, but they did not expect what happened next.

Christa, whom I had tried repeatedly to reach on the phone with no success, greeted me that morning with, 'Hello Mr Reed, we must improve our communications.' I looked at her in disbelief. 'I am sorry, it is too late for that,' I replied. When the resolution was put and defeated, Christa and Desmond looked nonplussed. I had eight times as many votes as they did.

Next came the resolution to re-elect them as directors. When we voted against it, effectively removing them from office immediately, there was total mayhem. Tom Sawyer brought the meeting to an abrupt close and a Granville Baird banker jumped to his feet. 'Lock the doors, no one must leave the room,' he declared dramatically. 'This is price sensitive, we need to ring the Stock Exchange and ask for the shares to be suspended.' With that, he ran out of the room to telephone the Stock Exchange. While we hung around, the directors went into a huddle. I dared not look at James or Tom Sawyer. I later learned that Christa and Desmond appeared to be in a state of shock.

Stock Exchange officials said they could see no reason why the shares should be suspended as long as shareholders were informed of what had taken place. A statement was rushed out on the RNS company alerts service that flashes up on the screens of everyone involved in financial services, including City journalists. That banker had been right about the effect on the share price; it went into free-fall, plunging 25 per cent in a day as shareholders struggled to make sense of what had happened.

The bankers forbade us to talk to the press that day. That was a mistake, because subsequently nobody really understood why I had acted as I had. We simply put out a statement saying that there had been a 'breakdown of trust'. I later spoke to the *Financial Times* and one or two other papers, but I did not see the need to go into detail. 'There is a complete breakdown of trust in Christa Echtle's and Desmond Doyle's corporate governance of Reed Health by major shareholders,' I told the *FT*. 'Quoting chapter and verse would be counter-productive at this stage.'

Christa and Desmond, now without jobs, rushed off to seek legal advice to see if they could overturn the vote. The problem for me was that some of the institutional share-holders, who had good relations with Christa and the press, were singing like canaries. I was portrayed as some kind of nut-case, but I knew exactly what I was doing. I simply was not prepared to let Christa run off with the company. I would do exactly the same again.

At Schroders, Andy Brough, whose fund held nearly 20 per cent of the shares, said: 'I have never seen anything like this in my fifteen years in the City.' Another investor said: 'It is outrageous. Whose interest is this guy acting in? This was done without consulting any of us.'

Of course it was; I could not risk warning them before-hand. In any case, to have done so would have been giving them insider information, which is against the law.

Andy Brough and Tim Steer began to tell the press that

they would call for an extraordinary general meeting (EGM) to reinstate Christa and Desmond. Obviously, they had not done their arithmetic. Andy Brough even rang James, saying, 'If you won't reinstate them, we will.'

What they may not have known then is that in addition to the shares I spoke for, which came to more than 50 per cent, James held a further 6 per cent which had not been used, so we had a clear majority.

We had agreed that James and I would be the only ones to talk to the press and City analysts, and even then, on a very limited basis. 'We are looking for guidance from the independent director,' Tim Steer told the London *Evening Standard*. 'It is time for Lord Sawyer to step up to the plate.' Tom, quite wisely, stayed out of the way. What could he say?

Faced with a vacuum on our side, the press began to speculate.

The *Standard*'s Robert Lea had grasped that we might be unhappy with the resolution regarding acquisitions, but could not resist suggesting that pure envy might be my prime motive for removing the chief executive and finance director.

'Reed Health had been having such a good run under Echtle's management that ... Reed Health was vastly outperforming its former parent company and was being valued on the stock market at almost twice the capitalisation of Reed Executive,' he wrote.

The share price may have been riding high, but the company, as we found when we took control back, was in a mess.

For a couple of weeks the newspapers ran stories about the threatened EGM, but once they did their sums, Brough,

Steer and others realised there was no point in demanding one. We held the majority of the shares and we did not want two people whom we considered over-ambitious running the company we owned. It was that simple. As I have said before, control is everything.

I cannot pretend this episode was not embarrassing for James, Derek and Tom Sawyer, but eventually they forgave me. It certainly put paid to the Starburst strategy. One shareholder said: 'Starburst is history. Nobody will take any shares from Alec Reed again.'

Two of Reed Health's non-executive directors resigned in protest, and Patience Wheatcroft was scathing in *Management Today*, as was the *Investors Chronicle*. Reed Health's shares continued to fall. The confrontation had been bruising all round, not to mention detrimental to our wallets.

* * *

The whole episode made us rethink the merits of Reed being a public company. At the same time, increasing regulation stemming from reports of various captains of industry, starting with Sir Adrian Cadbury, made running a public company increasingly onerous. Top managers spent far too much time talking to compliance officers about what they could and could not do. Then in 2003 came the Higgs Report into the role of non-executive directors, which proved the final straw.

The late Sir Derek Higgs, who was a friend and neighbour in the Cotswolds, had been an eminent investment banker at SG Warburg and went on to head the Prudential insurance group. Yet, despite a lifelong career in the City, he regarded business and businessmen with some suspicion. A lifelong *Guardian* reader who rode a motorbike, he was something of a maverick, and his report read as if he wanted to make the lives of public company directors as difficult as possible.

Among its stipulations were that independent non-executives should make up half of a board; that a chief executive should never move up to become chairman of the same company; and that there should be a 'senior' non-executive director. To be truly independent, non-executive directors should not come from the same business sector and should not stay on the board for more than nine years.

I had never been a fan of non-executive directors and only brought them on to our board to avoid trouble, but the idea of having to pay for another lot struck me as absurd. Although in theory boards could 'explain' why they were not complying, the Higgs code was effectively an edict.

Even so, I personally thanked Derek for putting blue water between entrepreneurs and public companies. My view is that entrepreneurs are simply not temperamentally suited to modern public company life.

The rules of the club I had joined in 1971 had changed beyond recognition. For the privilege of appearing on the share price pages of the *Financial Times* and being subject to intense scrutiny, we were paying almost £500,000 a year in administration and legal fees. We felt that money could be much better spent invested in the growth of reed.co.uk and Reed in Partnership.

After the Reed Health spin-off James took on new investment bankers at Altium who agreed with us that there was little point in staying a public company. Not only were we a family business wedded to organic growth, we also had no need for outside capital. Given the choice, I would have bought the company back long before, but it had been too expensive. One result of James spinning off Reed Health was to make Reed Executive smaller, and with the shares well below their high, we had the opportunity to take it private again.

Reed Executive was facing a cyclical downturn. As happens when the economy looks uncertain, demand for permanent jobs, particularly in accountancy and the financial services industry, had plunged, taking our profits with them.

In the financial year 2002, profits collapsed by 43 per cent to £8 million on sales of £349 million. Instead of grumbling, I had bought shares through the Reed Foundation whenever I thought they looked cheap. By 2002, the Foundation held about 18 per cent of Reed Executive. With the family stake, that added up 75 per cent, which meant we actually had to buy only the remaining quarter of Reed Executive, which we financed by a bridging loan.

On 5 April 2003, five months after I had ousted Christa and Desmond from Reed Health, the family launched an offer to buy back Reed Executive for 140p a share, valuing it at £62.6 million. Coincidentally it was the same day our soldiers went into Baghdad.

Led by our independent director Professor Michael Eysenck, the directors backed the takeover and we received 85 per cent irrevocable acceptances. Although the price was lower than the peak of 183p reached a couple of years previously, it was at an 18 per cent premium to the shares before the announcement of the offer. Nevertheless, there were a few snide comments. Patience Wheatcroft, now City

Editor of *The Times*, commented that we were 'unlamented', while the *Daily Telegraph* called the company an 'anachronism'. In 32 years we had never issued a share or made an acquisition. Well, I have always said that floating was our biggest mistake. We were lucky to be able to take the company back under family control where we can take a longer-term view.

Even so, I would point out that for much of our life as a public company our shares outperformed the FT 30 and then the FTSE 100 indices. Anyone investing at the start would have seen their money grow by 100 times at the peak.

At Reed Health we appointed one of the directors, David Fennel, as chief executive, but the company never regained momentum under him or his successor. We decided to bring it back into the fold, and in August 2005 James approached the then board with an offer for the company from James Reed & Partners, a vehicle formed originally to buy back Reed Executive. Somewhat to our surprise, they rebuffed us, so we were forced to launch a hostile bid of 55p a share, valuing the company at £38 million. In the end, Andy Brough at Schroder sold us his pivotal 19 per cent and Reed Health was once again under family control. James and his team have since rebuilt it into a fine company within the group.

Since 2003 James has continued to run Reed for the long term, and I know it is a relief for him to be out of the public company spotlight.

I remain Founder at Large, but in my later years I have taken great pleasure in finding new interests and challenges. One is Juxon Ltd, which owns all the farmland including the Kiddington estate of more than 1,600 acres in Oxfordshire, which we bought in 2010. Another is The Big Give.

CHAPTER 22

The Big Give

MY LATEST PASSION IS THE BIG GIVE. In 2007 I held a brainstorming session to explore how I could give away money more effectively and at the same time help others to do the same. Although I continued to support Ethiopiaid, Womankind and several other causes, I was struggling to find new charities in areas that truly interested me. I wanted to find a more intelligent way of giving money to charity.

I like to be pro-active about giving, and do not usually respond well to requests. Like most philanthropists, I receive sack-loads of letters from various charities and individuals, which usually end up in the bin, either because their literature is too long and tedious to read or because they operate in areas that do not fire my interest. Although I have had cancer twice and I love animals, I rarely support cancer or animal charities because I know they are already well endowed. Neither do I give to religious or political charities. As in business, I like to be in control.

I want to give intelligently and believe that most people feel the same way; they will give more if they can easily find a charity that truly engages them.

Guests at the round table discussion included some great philanthropic brains. There was Lord (Chris) Haskins, the former chief executive and chairman of Northern Foods; Lord Joffe, the founder of Hambro Life Insurance and former chair of Oxfam; Alex Jacobs, the director of Mango, which provides financial services to charities and NGOs; Michael Robson, the chief executive of Andrews Estate Agents, started by my hero Jackson-Cole; and Myles Wickstead, a former British ambassador to Ethiopia. Most of them had experience of working with charities in various places all over the world.

To start with, we kicked various ideas around, but made little headway. Then just as we were breaking up for lunch, Mike Robson, whom I know well, said almost as an aside: 'Well Alec, what you really need, of course, is a virtual charity.' Everyone nodded in agreement and we trooped down to the restaurant below the offices of Reed Learning where I was hosting the session. I was seated next to Mike at lunch, so I asked him, 'What the hell is a virtual charity?' He laughed and said he did not know, but felt instinctively that was what we needed.

I already had internet experience through reed.co.uk, so we decided that putting the details of charities online and offering a searchable website could be very appealing. We would make it easy to search for a charity in the way that reed.co.uk makes it easy to search for a job.

Jon Brooks at the Reed Foundation was working on the project and thought we would stimulate more interest if we asked the charities to nominate particular projects. So instead of just giving to Ethiopiaid, you could search the website to find one of its current projects that appealed to you.

The way it works is simple. On the Big Give website (the-biggive.org.uk) there is a map of the world on one side of the screen and a list of seven areas of interest, such as education or health, on the other. You can click on a region and then your area of interest.

For example, click on Africa and up will pop a long list of charities. You can then select a particular country and then choose a topic such as education. One example that will pop up is Book Aid, which gives books to schools and libraries in various African countries. If you click on its projects you will be able to choose 'Books Change Lives' in Cameroon or a number of other African states. If books don't flick your switch, you could try Jole Rider Friends, which supplies low-cost bicycles to help African children get to school. If neither of those appeals, there are a further 7,000 charities listed under 200 sectors, all detailing their own projects so that would-be donors can really drill down into specialist fields.

At the outset, we wanted donations of more than £100,000, which is why I called it The Big Give. Initially, I put in £1 million to help Jon get the website up and running. It took a lot of organisation and promotion. I also committed to give £1 million a year to various projects.

The first task was to interest charities to register on the site. We wrote an article for a charity magazine and I spoke about it at a big charity conference. When the charities contacted us, we explained what we were doing.

People who want to give to charity are often unsure about the efficiency of a particular organisation, so I insisted that charities must provide a lot of information to demonstrate that they were both reputable and efficient. One feature was that every charity should make its accounts available online through a link to the Charity Commission. That way, would-be donors could examine them. I also wanted the charities to make senior people available to meet donors. If individuals or companies are considering giving £100,000 to a charity, they need to know that it is well run and to be able to talk to someone in authority. Transparency is essential.

My idea was that donors could contact the charity of their choice through telephone numbers listed on the site. In the beginning we ran into problems because calls were going through to junior people at the charities who did not know about the Big Give site or were not sufficiently knowledgeable about their own charity. We then refined the process so that anyone calling would be put through to a designated senior person who would be briefed to talk to wealthy philanthropists.

We formally launched the idea to charities in October 2007 and within 24 hours several projects were each seeking £100,000. We could tell there was real excitement about the idea and within two months we had 1,000 charities wanting to register.

The next step was to promote the site to philanthropists. That was a bit trickier. I had a starter list of useful contacts, but we needed to extend well beyond that. The Association of Charitable Foundations understood what we were doing and helped us. We sent out marketing letters, made calls and so on, but getting people on board was hard work.

For the first year nothing much happened although we had a few successes. The Lancashire Wild Life Trust received a donation of £175,000 – a huge amount for such a small charity. The donor would never have heard about it had he not looked on the website. Overall though, the response was disappointing.

The charities said that insisting on big donations put people off; they were quite happy to ask for smaller sums. So we widened the scheme, but still the response was well below my hopes.

Then I had a brainwave. Why not try matched funding, where a donation is matched by someone else – so the charity receives double the original sum? It was not original – matched funding has been tried before, particularly in the United States, and often it does not increase donations by that much. What really works, I decided, was challenged matched funding – an offer to double the donation within a set time frame. There is nothing like a deadline to bring out people's competitive nature.

If I promised to put up £1 million to be available to double up any donation within 24 hours, would that encourage people to stump up? It was worth a try.

We sold the idea to the charities on the site and they told their regular donors about the scheme. Oxfam was particularly supportive, which impressed me. Such a big charity could have said, 'No thanks, we do our own marketing.'

With some trepidation, we launched the scheme on the site on 1 December 2008. Just 25 minutes later we had our 'Glastonbury moment' – the site crashed, unable to cope with the volume of responses. When we got it going again, it took just 20 minutes for the money to run out. I realised we were on to a winning formula. One donor told Jon Brooks that he was so inspired by the idea that he had doubled his original donation.

I felt The Big Give needed some gravitas behind it, so

I asked some famous people to lend their support. Lord Haskins and Lord Joffe had been at the original lunch and did not need asking twice. I also persuaded a further 25 well-known figures who are also philanthropists to join; many are also entrepreneurs. They include Charles Dunstone, the hugely successful founder of Carphone Warehouse, Michael Spencer of ICAP (the world's largest Inter-dealer broker), and Martha Lane-Fox. Others include Lord Bell, Martyn Lewis, Jon Snow and Frank Field, the Labour MP.

We experimented, and naturally some ideas failed. For example, I thought it might appeal to companies if instead of sending out the same bottles of champagne or cases of wine or hampers of delicacies to suppliers at Christmas, they sent charity vouchers instead. The idea was that the people who received them could 'spend' them on The Big Give. It would be a way of making people feel good at Christmas and spread the word about the pleasure of giving. Or so I thought.

We posted a £25 voucher to 10,000 businesses – a potential £250,000 for The Big Give. Sadly, only £8,000 worth was used. Either people did not understand the concept, or else they felt that their suppliers and contacts would prefer a bottle of champagne. But as I have said before, failure can be a valuable spur if you learn from it.

Matched challenged funding had been a great success, but for 2009 I wanted to make it more exciting. What we needed was a bigger pool of money to match donations. In America if someone is a trustee of a charity they are expected to support it – to stump up money: in the UK, however, trustees often feel it is enough to give their names and time to a cause.

I decided to try to change some minds, and approached the trustees of various charities to give us some funds for matching. This time I put up £1.5 million, and a further £3 million was donated. The trustees of the Royal Opera House were particularly generous.

So many people complained that they had missed out because the time window was so short that in 2009 we decided to release the funds for matching over five days. It worked like a charm, and we raised £8.5 million. One regular donor to the World Wildlife Fund gave 60 per cent more than in previous years.

In 2010 we again targeted wealthy charity trustees to put up money for the matching fund, and 318 charities joined the Christmas Big Give Challenge, which kicked off with a great party.

I love parties and know that every year the exclusive Piccadilly store Fortnum & Mason throws one for a thousand people to support a charity of its choice. So in 2010 James's wife Nicola approached Kate Weston Hobhouse, who runs Fortnum & Mason, to pitch the idea of making The Big Give the beneficiary. To my delight, she agreed. I suggested that we make the £50 entrance ticket double as a voucher for The Big Give. Quentin Blake, the artist and children's illustrator, agreed to design the tickets which, when the guests arrived, were exchanged for a Big Give voucher accompanied by instructions on how to use the site to donate to the charity of their choice. There was also a raffle – £10 bought guests a Christmas cracker with a £10 voucher inside. The first voucher was donated to The Big Give at 10 p.m. that evening by Cherie Blair. There was also an online auction featuring prizes such as Quentin Blake's original illustration for the invitation, a Fortnum's hamper and a walk-on part for a child in a pantomime.

Held over four floors of the store, the party was a great party despite the snow deterring some guests. The Paddington Academy choir sang carols as guests arrived and other festive music was performed by the National Children's Orchestra, the Classical Opera Company and Reed's own Mike Whittaker tickling the ivories on the second floor. As well as buffet food, free samples of Fortnum's own delicacies were available and the champagne flowed. By the end of the following week we had raised more than £9.5 million – and this at the tail end of the worst recession for 50 years.

The Big Give's raison d'être is to promote charitable giving and to make it fun. Targeting children is one way of achieving that, so we approached the Dragon School near Oxford. Knowing that this co-educational prep school is well known for its innovative approach to learning, we thought the head might be receptive. We were right. For Christmas 2010 we persuaded the parents to put up £1,000 to buy £5 vouchers to distribute to the pupils who then 'spent' their vouchers on the Big Give website. We continue to promote the idea among schools, and have added Westminster Under School, St Olaf's in Oxford and James Allen's Girls School in Dulwich. In the next couple of years we hope to have many more schools on board following an article in *The Economist* which has stimulated considerable interest.

When I won the Beacon Award for philanthropy in November 2010, I put the £30,000 prize into the Big Give matched-funding challenge, later turning it into £200,000 in December 2011. Martyn Lewis, the former BBC newscaster, hosted the awards and made a flattering speech about me.

In my response I naturally plugged The Big Give. 'It is not easy to give money away intelligently,' I said. 'The Big Give introduces intelligence into giving. I'm delighted to use the £30,000 as the catalyst for a £200,000 matched funding challenge on theBigGive.org.uk, to benefit the charities of other Beacon Prize winners.'

The run-up to the Christmas challenge and the Big Give party had an extra dimension for me as I was keeping a big secret. In mid-November I had received a letter from the Cabinet Office asking me if I would be willing to accept the honour of a Knight Bachelor for 'services to business and charity' in the 2011 New Year's honours list. It was a total surprise to me, although not to some of my friends and colleagues, as I later found out. Of course I replied that I would be delighted to accept. It is easy to be cynical about these kinds of honours until you are on the receiving end of them. Public recognition is immensely satisfying, and I had been very pleased to receive my CBE in 1994.

The prospect of a knighthood at the age of 76 felt a bit like an end-of-term prize! Adrianne was naturally very pleased for me, but, ever in search of a low profile, she said she would have preferred not to change her name to Lady Reed. I told her we would call her Lady Adie.

Once it was announced on New Year's Eve, I discovered that, unknown to me, Mike Whittaker had decided more than two years earlier to organise a formal nomination. The work in preparing it and gathering letters of support was done by Joanna Roberts, a young woman who joined Reed as a graduate trainee and later worked for Ethiopiaid, where she demonstrated her ruthless efficiency by organising one of our busiest trips ever to Ethiopia. I am obviously extremely grateful to both of them and to all those who provided letters of support. When the nomination was submitted in July 2008, they were told that if no honour had been offered within two years they could consider that the nomination had failed. So they were almost as surprised as I had been when the announcement came. We celebrated quietly, under siege due to the snow, with a drink with our old friends Geoff and Margaret Baker.

Receiving a knighthood sounds quite solemn, but I found it enormous fun. In the days that followed I was almost overwhelmed by the tidal wave of goodwill pouring into my home via letters, phone calls, emails and even texts. People I knew in the distant past have been in contact along with former Reed employees I had not heard news of for many years.

My brother John was the first to ring and congratulate me. In fact he was so overwhelmed with emotion he had to pass the phone to his wife, Jenny.

Our already busy social life went into overdrive, with a series of invitations to dinner parties from people who wanted to celebrate with us.

The investiture took place on 8 February 2011. Unlike the awarding of my CBE, when Alex was working for a charity in Belize, I was able to take her with me to the Palace. Adrianne naturally came too, along with Richard and James. Prince Charles had given me my CBE and once again he did the honours.

Outside we took some photographs of our own to add to the official pictures before celebrating over lunch at the Ritz. I still have to pinch myself sometimes to make sure I am really awake and not dreaming.

CHAPTER 23

Endgame

SUCCESSFUL PRACTITIONERS OF 'PEOPLISM' become capitalists. If a boss picks the best people and then trains and nurtures them as I suggest in my book *Capitalism Is Dead: Peoplism Rules*, the company will become prosperous and the owners will accrue capital. Then they can buy farmland! At least that is what I do.

I am not a fan of the stock market; for me farmland is the perfect investment. It is relatively stable, its value has risen from £1,000 an acre to £6,000 in the past two decades, and the pleasure of owning is thrown in for free – riding my horse Ben over my own land on a Saturday morning gives me a huge kick. Although I say that floating Reed was my biggest mistake, I also know that I could never have bought my farm at Little Compton without the proceeds. The appreciation in land values has been some compensation for selling a third of the company too cheaply and, above all, it has given me great joy.

For some time, I had been looking for more farmland to buy, and instructed Sam Butler of the agents Butler Sherborn to keep his eyes open for me. He suggested a few deals and we bought some of them, but most were smaller than I wanted. Then, in September 2009, an opportunity to buy an estate just half an hour away from Little Compton came up. It was unique and too good to resist.

Kiddington Hall and the surrounding 2,000-acre Oxfordshire estate came on the market in an unusual way. The previous owner, Maurice Robson, a City millionaire and son of the founder of Robson Rhodes, was forced to sell it to fund his divorce settlement. He was devastated. He had inherited it from his father, who had paid about £115,000 for the house and estate in 1950. On the other hand, I was delighted with the opportunity to own it.

Kiddington Hall is a Grade-II listed stately home, built in 1673, with landscaped gardens designed by 'Capability' Brown. The asking price for the house and the entire estate was £42 million. Lovely though the hall is, I am not interested in grand houses; I am more than happy living in our converted cottages in Little Compton and our two-bedroom house in Kensington.

Clearly aware that £42 million was a huge sum to ask, particularly after the 2008 crash, the selling agents Strutt & Parker divided the estate into ten lots. Lot 1 was Kiddington Hall and roughly 400 acres of land that went with it. The other 1,600 acres of arable farmland and properties had been divided into nine separate lots, and I instructed Sam to buy all nine. I believe there were no other offers for the whole nine lots.

The hall was sold to Jemima Khan, daughter of the late Sir James Goldsmith and former wife of the Pakistan cricketer Imran Khan, so the newspapers were naturally far more interested in that story than in my purchase.

Most of the 36 houses or barns in the village of Kiddington that go with the land are let. I have no interest in becoming a landlord with tenants and houses to look after, although I will, of course, treat the current tenants with respect as long as their leases last. But we are in the process of doing up the houses as they become vacant and selling them. One of my ideas is to turn southern Kiddington into an equestrian estate – rather like a residential golf course. The people who bought the houses could keep their horses at the stables and go riding whenever the mood took them. They could then enjoy some of the most beautiful scenery in the world. That is one idea. Meanwhile, we are selling the properties off as the leases come up for renewal. Kiddington is a classic Cotswolds village. I love the land and I am excited at the prospect of improving it.

* * *

Occasionally people ask how I would like to be remembered. I hope people will remember me as both entrepreneurial and lucky – someone who laughed a lot and attempted to improve the lives of others.

I do not just mean the poor in Africa, the abused women to whom Womankind has restored dignity or the previously unemployed for whom we have found permanent jobs. I also mean those rich people suffering from financial obesity. I hope I have been able to direct their giving in a more fulfilling way and to introduce them to charities with which they feel a strong bond but which they might never have encountered were it not for The Big Give.

I hope that some people who read this book will realise

that out of failure great things can come and being entrepreneurial can open many doors. Making money has given me the ability to take part in games that before I could only have dreamed of. Games of bidding for whole villages, starting new charities and supporting artistic endeavour.

Above all, I hope they will think of me as an ideas man. They may not like all my ideas – abandoning libraries in schools did not meet with much approval, for instance – but I hope some will be appreciated. May I never wake up in the morning without some new, probably wacky, but possibly world-beating idea fizzing in what my children call my 'amazing' brain. But don't ask me the date of the Battle of Waterloo.

Acknowledgements

Thank you to Judi Bevan for all the time and trouble she has taken in presenting my story as interestingly as she has. I fear that once or twice I appear to be immodest: I apologise for that, but my defence is that it is a result of the process.

There are a good number of people who have contributed enormously to my wellbeing who have not been named. They know who they are, but more importantly I do as well, and I am grateful to them all.

Index

Index